The NET-HEAD HANDBOOK

THE FIRST GUIDE TO COMPUTER *Chic*

BY NICK ROSEN

Cartoons by Stan Eales

Design by Stewart Larking

Web site: http://www.net-head.com

Acknowledgements

Many people helped me when I was a Newbie, giving freely of their time and resources to the painful task of making me partially computer literate.

I would like to thank Peter Kirstein, Jon Crowcroft, Angela Sasse and Mark Handley of University College London; Peter Dawe of Pipex; Peter Cochrane and Jeremy Barnes of BT Advanced Research Labs; Ian Cameron, Nigel Titley and Jag Minhas of BTnet; Mark Humphrey of Orange Plc; Russell Brady of Apple Computer; Tim O'Reilly of O'Reilly Associates; Anna Russell and Tom Donnelly of IBM; Martin Turner of CompuServe; Richard Rosen of Pritchard Corporate Finance; Sara Herscher-Shorland of Toshiba; Jonathan Miller of Delphi; Nick Leteny and Will Howell of ICLnet; Nick Passmore of *The Guardian*; Graeme Davies of Demon/Easynet; Gordon Joly of the BBC Multimedia Unit; Tim Leighton-Boyce of State 51; and Eva Pascoe of Cyberia. David Macmillan and Mal Peachey gave me the encouragement I needed to start work on the book.

My particular thanks to Mark Dziecielewski, Technical Director of Intervid. Without him I would have remained a permanent Newbie. He may not be responsible for the content of this book, but he is certainly to blame for my continuing presence in Cyberspace.

Thanks also to my editor Simon Prosser, illustrator Stan Eales and designer Stewart Larking and also Allison Greenaway.

The following were researchers/contributors on the Net-head Handbook: Debbie Barham, David Merrin, Zoe Baxter and Jo Hodges.

Contents

Introduction

The Internet is the fastest-growing social phenomenon on the planet. It has emerged from nowhere to become one of the icons of the 90s alongside child-waif models, global warming and the end of the Cold War.

When Henry Ford founded his company a century ago he predicted that cars would first be mocked and derided, then denounced, and finally everybody would want one. The same three-stage process is true of the Internet. The early 90s saw the "old-media" (print and TV) scoffing at this nerd's paradise. In 1995 the critics moved on to the problems of policing the Net – preventing copyright infringement, and pornography and criminality of every sort. The Internet just kept growing – at the rate of 10% per month. Now there are at least 40 million e-mail accounts. Soon everyone will want one.

This is the first style guide to the Net – an essential toolkit for locating yourself, and those you know, in the social whirl of cyberspace. It is not a technical guide, but it will help you understand the people who use the Net. It is an early map, charting the actual reality of virtual space.

In the near future the Internet will be all gizmos in one – your phone, fax, copier, radio, TV and video, library, shopping mall, newspaper, bank teller, accountant, alarm clock, diary, game-opponent, airline booking clerk, and food delivery service.

Even the most computer-illiterate and techno-fearing will have to stop worrying and learn to love the Net. So put on your anorak, practice hunching your shoulders and staying up at a keyboard all night. You too can become a

NET-HEAD

Chapter

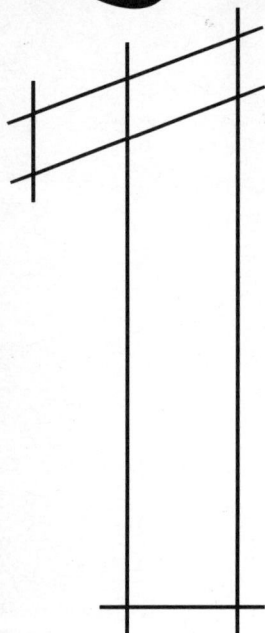

By their modems you shall know them

What is a Net-head?
Who is not a Net-head
Top ten ways to tell a Net-head
Why 'Net-head'?
Proud to be a Net-head
Net-heads are everywhere

What is a Net-head?

Net-heads are everywhere. They include farmers, bankers, scientists, gamers, ravers, dealers, healers, sci-fi fans, students, groupies, gropers, hippies, politicians, soldiers, writers, hacks, blacks, punks, monks, hunks, fraudsters, hackers, crackers, slackers, hobbyists, lobbyists, spies, gays, straights, bis, trilateralists, subgenii and trekkies, to name just a few.

As a result there is no one definition of 'Net-head'. There are only a variety of giveaway signs (see 'Top ten ways to tell a Net-head').

Who is not a Net-head

It is much easier to say who is not a Net-head.

Someone who uses their computer for spreadsheets, game-playing or database management but doesn't spend any time online is not a Net-head. Someone who has an e-mail address but does not use it is not a Net-head. Only if you at least log on and answer your e-mail can you really call yourself a Net-head.

Net-heads meet on the Internet – also known as Cyberspace, the Dataverse, the Electrosphere and the Information Superhighway. It is nothing less than the hard-wiring of the entire planet. One day the Net will connect the world together. In 1991 it was still a text-only community. By 1995 pictures had become a part of Net-life. By1999 it will not be necessary to spell, or even speak English, to be a Net-head.

Net-heads have added a computer-life to their social life. For them, a meeting of minds is a meeting of modems. They are their own society: a literate, hyper-informed underground that is rapidly becoming mainstream.

The Net is where Net-heads send mail, play games, do research, carry on affairs and appear to be anyone or anything they want to other Net-heads. They can walk tall (if they are disabled), contribute to discussions on subjects they know nothing about or play games against total strangers.

Why say 'Net-head'?

The word 'Net-head' has caught on because it sounds better than most of the alternatives. The impersonal word 'users' has unpleasant connotations of addiction or psychological neediness. Calling them 'Netizens' smacks of school and constitution lessons. 'Net-head' is more universal and more flexible.

Net-head can also be used as a verb. 'To Net-head' is to waste time in front of a keyboard, although it also applies to the work of Net-based research and reading mail and news. Net-heading often consumes many hours, even if the intention was to 'just log in and check my mail'. It is time which non-Net-heads would prefer to spend meeting other people or even just curled up in front of the TV.

Proud to be a Net-head

There are companies called 'Net-head' everywhere from London to New York to Sydney, offering Internet services (part of a new boom industry). There is a cartoon called Net-head (TM). There is an anonymous diarist called Annette Head, who writes about the activities of 'portly Cliff Stanford', owner of Demon Internet, the UK's largest Internet provider.

A search using Digital Computers' Alta Vista search engine revealed dozens of individuals who have chosen independently to list themselves as Net-heads on the Internet. Among others, there was this Cyberpunk from California:

```
> User-id: Nethead. Name: Auzie Morgan. Sex:
Male. Birthdate:
> 09/30/70. City: colton. State: CA. Registry
Questions. Favorite
> Movie?: Johny Mneumonic. Favorite Style of
Music?: Rage.
> Favorite Hobby?: Robotics/Skating/
Technology. Occupation?: Tech
> Support...
> http://topgun.cinecom.com/DPI/c0060000.HTM -
size 999 bytes -
> 10 Dec 95
>
```

Auzie appears a positive literati compared to Net-cadet Domol from Poland:

```
> * DOMOL *
> YO ! Welcome, you Nethead !!! If you HATE
things like: exams &
> kujing, smokers & cigarets. disco & polo.
etc... this are pages
> FOR YOU. But, if you LOVE: girls, spotrs.
good music, ME, mud.
> this are pages ESSPECIALY FOR YOU !!! Domol.
Obrazki. Proby...
> http://www.mat.uni.torun.pl/~domol/ - size
673 bytes - 4 Dec 95
>
```

There is the evangelistic Net-head TV:

```
Nethead T.V. is On!
> Nethead T.V. is a 60 second Quicktime video
which
> should be playable by any Macintosh, or
Windows machine using
> Quicktime for Windows. If you'd like more
details on Quicktime
> click here. Because we wanted to keep the
quality we sacrificed
> the bandwidth...
> http://203.19.76.57/tv/tv1.html - size 2K -
28 Nov 95
```

Net-heads are everywhere

Yes, Net-heads are everywhere. Cellphone modems have put the phone inside the computer. And solar-powered laptops are eliminating another piece of socket-dependence – the electricity supply.

That search for a phone-socket was why they were sometimes called the 'wired generation'. But 'wired' is becoming a rather tired word, and an irrelevant one. Increasingly we will connect via infra-red or satellite or radio-phone services like Ionica, a new company that's challenging BT for a slice of the UK home phone market.

The Net-head community accepts people from all walks of life as long as they have access to the Net and the skill to use it.

Many Net-heads are technical wizards and love computers, but not all. Some just know enough to read their e-mail or play their favourite MUD – multi-user dimension (q.v.).

The unwritten rule, until now, has been that wit, originality and even eccentricity are good and that sheeplike conformity and plain ignorance are bad. Net-heads are leading the change in the way we behave from one audience of millions to millions of audiences of one.

Although some Geeks are Net-heads, they are not identical. A Geek has no social skills and is usually obsessed with science or technology. Net-heads are more computer/telecom-specific. Geeks are known for their poor dress sense – lab coats would not be out of place among a party of them in college. Net-heads have no single style – they are too diverse. But they do have style. They have in common that they tend to invent their own dress code rather than following the dictates of the fashion press.

TOP TEN WAYS TO TELL A...
NET-HEAD

№10. Favourite chat-up line: 'What's your e-mail address?'

№9. Asks if he can 'just plug the laptop in' to your phone socket

№8. Always complaining about his phone bills

№7. Stays up all night and doesn't get drunk

№6. Wears an anorak indoors

№5. Eats junk food and drink lots of black coffee

№4. Lacking in social skills

№3. Has a celebrity mouse mat

№2. Has his e-mail address printed on his T-shirt

№1. Always knows where the nearest Cybercafe is

Chapter 2

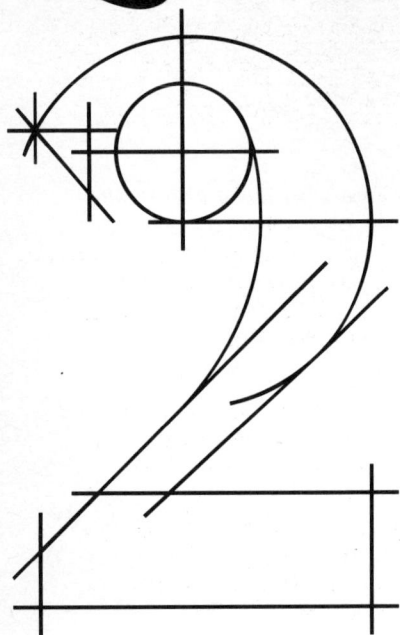

The eight types of Net-head

**Old Net-heads and New Net-heads – their share of the Internet population
Newbies and Net-cadets,
Netropolitans and Net-vets,
Profiteers and Cyberpunks,
Evangelists and Geeks
The Masters of the Dataverse**

New Net-heads for Old

After years of research we have established the eight basic Net-head categories amidst the diversity. Net-heads divide into two camps:

1. The New Net-head – part of the wave of Net-enthusiasm that has swept the world since approximately 1993, when pictures first came to the Internet.

2. The traditional, or Old Net-head – a member of the community that has been on the Net for approaching two decades.

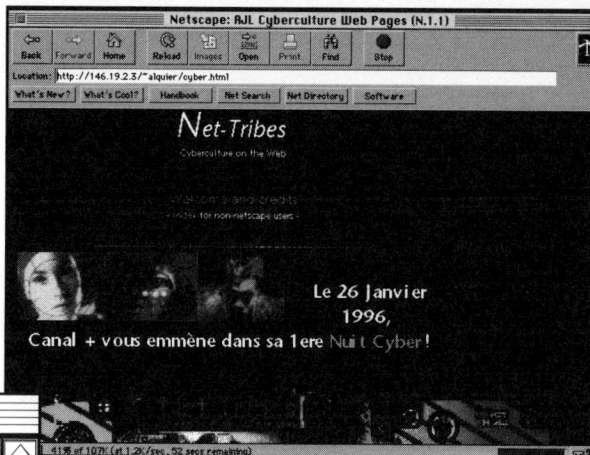

Netscape: AJL Cyberculture Web Pages (N.1.1)

Back Forward Home Reload Images Open Print Find Stop

Location: http://146.19.2.3/~alquier/cyber.html

What's New? What's Cool? Handbook Net Search Net Directory Software

Net-Tribes
Cyberculture on the Web

Le 26 Janvier
1996,
Canal + vous emmène dans sa 1ere Nuit Cyber !

The NET-HEAD HANDBOOK

NET-HEAD category	NET-HEAD stereotype	% of 40m total	Main distinguishing feature
new	newbies	25%	They know nothing
new	net-activists	15%	The world must be told
new	net-cadets	10%	Age less than 16
new	net-profiteers	10%	Make money fast!!!
new	netropolitans	5%	The new global elite
trad	net-veterans	15%	The cyberguides
trad	geeks	10%	Hate the new popularity
trad	cyberpunks	5%	Anarchists of the net

TOTAL 95%
The Net is always changing

Mr & Mrs Newbie

represent the fastest growing segment of the Net-head population – the middle-class non-specialists who are beginning to use the Net because it seems like a good idea. White in collar, if not in colour, some Newbies remain bewildered by the whole thing for their entire Net-head careers. But most graduate to other forms of Net-headness.

There are hundreds of thousands of e-mail accounts in British companies that are used by people who do not realise they are even on the Internet. In 1996 the Newbies are 80% male and mostly in the 30-45 age group. These guys are the ones that have the 'kit' to be on the Internet and have something useful they can do when they get there (i.e. communicate with other executives worldwide and do research – as well as be entertained).

The Newbies know nothing. Many don't really know why they're on the Internet. Mr Newbie is one of the 30% of the Internet audience who go online mainly for entertainment.

Geek Rating ▯

Chic Rating 😎 😎 😎

The Net-Activist

She knows exactly why she is on the Internet. She learns fast because she has a purpose. Some passionate interest, whether in human rights or bee-keeping or transvestism, spurs her on to amazing feats of technical prowess.

Geek Rating

Chic Rating

The Net-Cadet

He knows more than his parents and learns so fast it's frightening. He has a long-suffering tolerance of parental inability to do the simplest thing on a computer.

The Newbies' only hope of learning how to use the net is to listen to the Net-cadet. But if they do not have a 10-year-old to hand, they will have to turn for help to the Net-vet.

Geek Rating

Chic Rating

The Net-Vet

A kindly soul who will answer any question from anyone on the Internet however ignorant they are and however many times he has answered it before. It is Norbert the Net-vet who most reflects the founding spirit of the Internet – worldwide co-operation, subsidised by the taxpayer, with no thought of profit.

Geek Rating

Chic Rating

However hard they try to stick to Net etiquette (netiquette, *q.v.*), the Newbies are harassed and taunted by...

The Geek

An Internet fundamentalist, a purist. He believes he is defending the Net, which is being transformed by its new popularity. He looks ugly and is often spotty after years being irradiated by computer screen gamma-rays. There are millions of Geeks around the world who prefer text-only Internet. A sense of

snobbish pride prevents them from switching to the graphical interfaces on the World Wide Web that are standard for new Net-heads and are the reason for the Internet's rapid growth.

Help is on the way. The Newbie is being joined by other, more capable newcomers – Net-head types who master the technology at a single leap. The Newbie can do his Christmas shopping thanks to the next species of Net-head.

Geek Rating

Chic Rating

The Net-Profiteers

The young industry has already spawned many millionaires. Net-Profiteers is the name the Geeks give them. It is unfairly pejorative. After all, the profit motive is now driving the growth of the Internet, which began life as an academic experiment. But the anti-commercial element is still the dominant one. Most people won't pay for anything on the Net.

Geek Rating

Chic Rating

The Cyberpunk

is the true anarchist of the Internet: his natural enemies are the Geeks and the Profiteers. Cyberpunks believe the Net is for anybody to do anything with. Cyberpunks' favourite saying is 'Information wants to be free'. They think everything on the Internet should be free – and the Profiteers hate that. Some Cyberpunks also have the power to get around passwords and other toll-stations on the info-hiway. They are often detected and stopped by the Geeks, most of whom are computer systems operators. Despite his rock-star good looks, Malcolm the Cyberpunk would rather stay at the keyboard and try to hack in to the Mir Spacestation than go out with the lads.

Geek Rating

Chic Rating

There are stars in TRW (The Real World) and there are Internet stars, also known as Net-gods. Occasionally the two categories intersect – as in the

case of actor Stephen Fry, who published his own Web page while 'on the run' from the media in 1995. Stephen Fry is a Netropolitan.

The Netropolitans

are a new planetary elite of laptop-packing air-travellers. They have an Internet account at home and one in the country they visit most often. They also have an account with a global provider like CompuServe or Microsoft or IBM or Planet Internet, so wherever they are in the world their e-mail is only a local call away.

Geek Rating 💾 💾 💾
Chic Rating 😎 😎 😎 😎

THE MASTERS (AND MISTRESSES) OF THE DATAVERSE, aka…

the Net GODS

Geeks

Peter Dawe – the first person to make money from the Net
Prof. Peter Kirstein – the first Brit on the net
Jack Schofield – computer journalist
Douglas Adams – *Hitchhiker's Guide*
Eva Pascoe – unintelligible Polish accent, must be an intellectual
Paola Katuria, Internet Consultant

Net-Vets

Al Gore – if the Internet was a country,
Gore would be President
David Shaw MP – evidence that some
Net-heads are social misfits
Odd de Presno, founder of Kidnet
Jon Crowcroft, Professor of bigger, wider, deeper at UCL
Nigel Titley, BT, master Internet builder
Davey Winder, *Sunday Times* lickspittle
Nicholas Pioch – the Web Louvre
Tim Berners-Lee – inventor of the World Wide Web
Alla Main, crazy name, crazy woman
Roger Green, *Internet* Magazine
Jonathan Newby – Publisher, IPC New Media

Cyberpunks

Tim Boyce, State 51
Cynthia Rose, new-age journalist
Dan O'Brien, Internet insultant
The Shamen – the most active band on the Internet
Heath Bunting, artist and garbagologist
Daniel Pemberton, ambient technomusician
Robert Lord, IUMA
Buggy G. Riphead – Netographer
Courtenay Inchbald – Punk in a suit

Newbies

Prince, who announced his marriage on the Net
Jonathan Ross – the archetypal Newbie
Ian Taylor MP, Minister for Cyberspace 1994-?
Geoff Hoon MP, Shadow Minister for Cyberspace 1995-?
Anne Taylor MP – known to her friends as 'My First Web Page'
Peter Cochrane, head of research, BT –
the professional Newbie
Ian Hislop, *Private Eye* Editor
Keilish Patel, Cyberspy Cafe

Net-Profiteers

Bill Gates, bill@msn.net
Jonathan Miller (not the doctor, the other one)
Tony Wilson, Factory Records
Ivan Pope, *3W Magazine*
Jeremy Silver, head of EMI Interactive

Robert Deveraux – Net Virgin
Pierce Casey – Mayfair On-line

Net-Activists

Tony Blair MP, who thinks the Internet is 'fascinating'
Kathy Newton, Fried Green Tomatoes Cafe, Northampton
James Coates, Demon salesman with a mission to explain
Kashka – proud to be a dog
Keith Teare – Channel Cyberia and the SWP
Jo Boatman – Cyberian TV
Mark O'Conor – Bird & Bird

Netropolitans

Stephen Fry
Tim O'Reilly
Madonna
Mick Jagger
Billy Idol
Herbie Hancock
Brian Eno
William Latham

Chapter 5

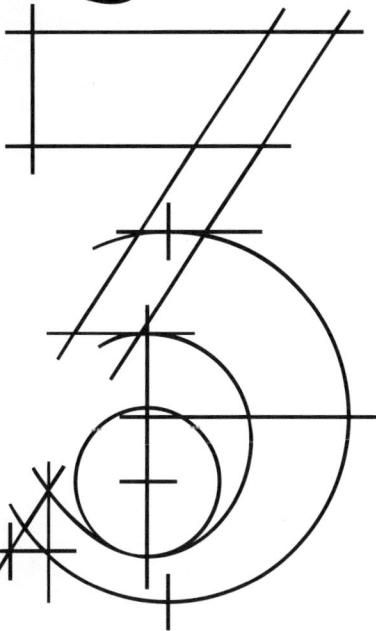

MEET THE NET-HEADS

Top ten ways to tell a Newbie
Mr Newbie – Everyman on the Internet
The Internet saves a life
Top ten ways to tell a Net-vet
Norbert – the ever-helpful Vet
Top ten ways to tell a Profiteer
Vanessa Fox – PR woman
Top ten ways to tell a Net-cadet
Bert the Net-cadet – the junior Net-head
Scouts sell cookies on the Internet
Top ten ways to tell a Net-activist
Hettie the student – fighting sexist stereotyping
Top ten ways to tell a Cyberpunk
Malcolm – aka the Cardinal – his hacker handle
Top ten ways to tell a Geek
Howard the Geek
Top ten ways to tell a Netropolitan
Charles the Netropolitan
Is the Queen a Net-head?

TOP TEN WAYS TO TELL A...
NEWBIE

10. Has many opinions about the Internet but has not actually used it

9. Doesn't know how to programme the video

8. Only has one phone line

7. Says things like 'Did you get my e-mail?'

6. Begins IRC sessions with the words 'Is this thing working?'

5. Searches Yahoo for the word 'sex'

4. Posts Usenet messages like 'Where can I get software for my Amiga?'

3. Spends more time phoning technical support than actually online

2. Has an e-mail address like aol.com or compuserve.com

1. Sends e-mails like 'This is a test'

Mr Newbie was one of those people who would always be a Newbie. No matter how long he tried to master the intricacies of computing and the Internet, he would never be at ease with the technology. Because he could just about understand the simple menu on his screen at work, Mr Newbie deluded himself that he knew all about computers. No amount of painful and time-wasting experience dented his blind self-confidence or his hopeless ignorance.

His boss was even more ignorant than he, which helped insulate him against the obvious criticisms that could have been made. His boss looked on keyboards as below his status. The secretary dealt with all the office e-mail, but for some reason Mr Newbie never could get around to asking her for help.

Just as well he never suffered a stroke online. His would not have been one of those net-miracles.

AUDIO SPEAKERS NOT WORKING DUE TO COMPATIBILITY PROBLEMS

BIG, LOW PRICE IBM COMPUTER

SILLY MOUS MAT

U.S. ROBOTICS MODEM

ONE PHONE LINE SO HIS FRIENDS GET ANNOYED

WRIST IN A
SLING FROM RSI

PUZZLED
EXPRESSION

BOTTLE OF HOT
SAUCE THAT HE
BOUGHT BY
ACCIDENT WHEN HE
WAS TRYING OUT
SECURE ORDERING
FORM

CD ROM
GAMES THAT
DON'T WORK

SEAT TOO HIGH
OR TOO LOW
FOR DESK

DUMMIES GUIDE
TO THE INTERNET

NORBERT THE NET-VET

TOP 10 WAYS TO TELL A...
NET-VET

10. His phone line is permanently engaged between the hours of 8pm and 4am

9. Spends hours tinkering with his software

8. At social functions he introduces his wife as 'my domain server' and his children as 'my client application'

7. When you ask him his address it begins 'http://www...'

6. Wears criss-cross pattern sweaters from M&S

5. Has a Web site with no graphics

4. Uses Net-acronyms like IMHO (in my humble opinion) even in ordinary conversation

3. Two words – 'draw-string hood'

2. Apart from his wife, the only other women in his life have names with @ in the middle

1. Shudders visibly when you mention the words 'Windows 95'

The backbone of the Internet is the network of wide-bandwidth cables that connects the world's biggest Internet computers. But the real backbone of the Internet is the network of kindly enthusiasts who think the world's problems can be solved by computer networks. Take Norbert, a charter member of the Internet Engineering Task Force. His calling card carries his e-mail address and (the latest status symbol) his ISDN phone number. Aged 36, with a pot belly, thinning hair, dandruff, thick glasses and shoulders as round as boulders from his years at the screen, Norbert met his wife in a commune in Devon. They live on pulses and macrobiotic food.

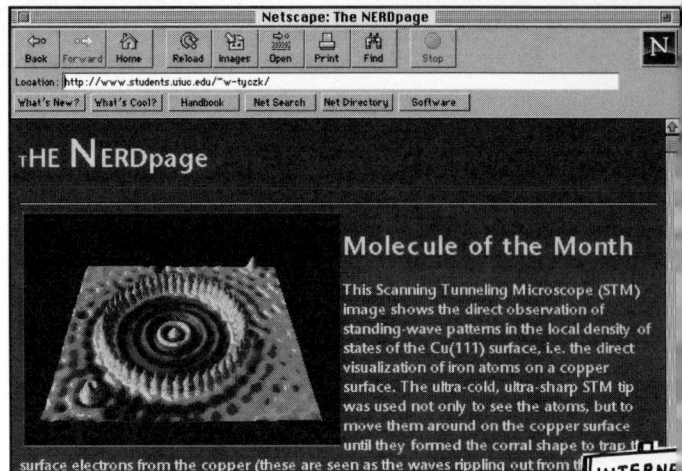

Netscape: The NERDpage

Back Forward Home Reload Images Open Print Find Stop

Location: http://www.students.uiuc.edu/~w-tyczk/

What's New? What's Cool? Handbook Net Search Net Directory Software

тHE NERDpage

Molecule of the Month

This Scanning Tunneling Microscope (STM) image shows the direct observation of standing-wave patterns in the local density of states of the Cu(111) surface, i.e. the direct visualization of iron atoms on a copper surface. The ultra-cold, ultra-sharp STM tip was used not only to see the atoms, but to move them around on the copper surface until they formed the coral shape to trap the surface electrons from the copper (these are seen as the waves rippling out from th...

He operates his computer sittting cross-legged on the floor. If you need information Norbert will always give it to you. He knows it is worth money, but he is motivated by a spirit of sharing the vast array that is the Internet. This is the saving grace of the Net as far as the Profiteers are concerned. It means they can draw on years of expertise for the cost of a phone call. People like Norbert do not even expect to be wined and dined in hip restaurants. Their only drawback is that they think that discussions about bandwidth and hardware are fascinating and they will answer many questions they have not even been asked… at great length.

Bytes
>>> INTERNET SAVES A LIFE

A Scot who had an epileptic attack while chatting on-line found a lifesaver in cyberspace – who phoned across the Atlantic for an ambulance.

Richard Eastman of Massachusetts, who manages a forum on genealogy over CompuServe, said that he acted after he noticed some odd messages from one of about 20 computer users during a late night, regular weekly session.

First the user reported that he didn't feel good, and then he typed 'Something funny is going on.'

Eastman had never heard of the man and was unsure if the messages were a hoax, but a nurse from New York immediately began asking the Rev. Kenneth Walker in Scotland for his symptoms. 'He was having great difficulty typing on his keyboard. We all make errors... but he was making gross errors, which made it seem more real', Eastman said.

At one point Walker wrote 'By keyboatd it melting ... I jest nuut.' Minutes later he typed 'Helo ... have broblemd ,,, thimk I am waying stroke.'

Eastman then started asking him for his phone number. After six attempts he finally got the number, called a telephone operator and quickly found himself talking to a police officer in Scotland.

The police forced their way into Walker's home minutes after Eastman called and took him to a hospital where he was treated and eventually released.

Walker later phoned Eastman to thank him. He said doctors believed his attack was triggered by his flickering computer screen.

Eastman, who has written a book about genealogy, and Walker, considered an expert on Scottish records and archives, have since found they have many things in common. 'It's kind of an interesting thing how two lives 3,000 miles apart get wrapped up', Eastman said.

COMPUSERVE: GO GENEALOGY

TOP TEN WAYS TO TELL A...
NET-PROFITEER

10. When the bill comes she asks the restaurant manager if he wants a home page on the Internet

9. Reads alt.sex newsgroup to get a sense of the latest Internet marketing ideas

8. Takes her laptop with her on a date

7. If someone propositions her on the Net she doesn't complain – she just asks them to send her an airline ticket

6. Has her Web page address on her engraved letterhead

5. Has a photo of herself together with Bill Gates

4. Has Aveda and Mr Fish on her list of favourite links

3. Has a free e-mail account

2. Says things like 'The Net's all very well, but nobody's making any money out of it'

1. Invites Net-veterans back to her place for a night-cap and then gets them to fix her computer

Vanessa Fox – PR woman

Vanessa sees the Internet as a great way of making money and has already written a book 'The Internet: A Great Way Of Making Money', which led to her being flamed in several thousand different newsgroups and having to change her e-mail address.

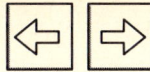

This was exactly the sort of publicity she hoped to achieve. Like the legendary Canter and Siegel, a husband and wife legal team who published a best-selling book on the back of their Net-unpopularity, she thought this would make her name and her fortune.

She spends a large part of each day sitting in front of the computer in full make-up, heels and a crumpled Donna Karan suit. Her most exciting fashion discovery of the year was a Prada bag that was exactly the right size for a Compaq Aero.

The Net-Cadet

TOP TEN WAYS TO TELL A...
NET-CADET

10. Has an overdeveloped right hand from driving the joystick
9. Knows all the characters from DOOM
8. Types with one finger
7. Says things like 'Hard-wiring the planet is an awfully big adventure'
6. Prefers the X-files to Power Rangers
5. Beats his dad at noughts and crosses
4. Wants to be a programmer when he grows up
3. Is in love with a 12-year-old girl in New York
2. Tests games for computer magazines
1. Charges his dad £10 an hour to fix his computer

Mr Newbie turns to his son Bert, aged 12 and annoyingly precocious. Bert is fluent on any piece of technology you care to name – probably including the Ford Sierra, which he has driven several times without his parents' knowledge. Bert's favourite part of the Net is games, but he likes exploring the whole thing.

At school, where all the kids are computer literate, parents with Internet connections are still an elite. Most of the boys with

Bytes
>>>SCOUT'S SELL COOKIES ON THE INTERNET

The Boston area council of the Girl Scouts has launched a sales campaign on the World Wide Web. Girl Scouts have been selling cookies since 1934. Seventy-five girls aged 14 to 16 are involved in operating the store. The Cookie Store Web site provides complete product descriptions of the eight types of cookies, including nutritional values and pricing and ordering instructions. Customers click on the type of cookie desired — Thin Mints, Do-Si-Do peanut butter cookies or another favourite — and enter the number of boxes to be shipped and complete billing information (credit cards are accepted). Cookies are delivered via United Parcel Service. Girl Scout officials said the program was designed to teach the young entrepreneurs the techniques of merchandising and fund-raising.

http://cookies.openmarket.com/GSstore

SCRAP OF PAPER
CONTAINING THE CODE
TO GET AROUND SURFWATCH

COPY OF
SURFWATCH
SO HE CAN'T
SEE BANNED
SIGHTS

BASEBALL
JACKET

SEAT WITH
CUSHION SO HE
CAN USE HIS DAD'S
COMPUTER

BABY
PHONE

LITTLE
NOTEBOOK
WITH WEB
ADDRESSES

GAME JOYSTICK
(DRIVES HIS DAD
MAD BECAUSE HE
DOESN'T KNOW HOW
TO UNPLUG IT AND
PUT THE MOUSE BACK
IN THE SOCKET)

access compete with each other to outwit SurfWatch, the software the school has recommended all parents should install on their hard drive to prevent kids from accessing porn on the World Wide Web. Danny, the biggest Geek in Bert's year, has hacked the source code and obtained the master list of banned addresses, many of them quite mundane.

Bert's best friend at school is Betty – who, despite being a girl, had been known to beat him at Ridge Racer. His favourite poster is Organic TV by William Latham, which is on his bedroom wall along with pin-up photos of dinosaurs and Beavis and Butthead.

The Net-Activist

TOP TEN WAYS TO TELL A...
NET-ACTIVIST

10. Has single-issue campaign stickers all over the computer
9. Says things like 'Shell are *really* messing up the rainforest near Guyacil... that's in deepest Ecuador'
8. Dating a guy she met in the Rainbow Cafe Internet tent at the Glastonbury festival

7. Will sleep with anyone from Santa Cruz
6. Wears DMs and clothes from charity shops
5. Smokes roll-ups
4. Orders her food from health food shops by e-mail
3. Beat the guys at computer games
2. Appears on TV programmes about freedom of speech on the Internet
1. Spends more time networking than actually getting anything done

HETTIE THE NET-ACTIVIST – FIGHTING AGAINST STEREOTYPING

Hettie, a German studying at the University of North London, joined the Net because it was a re-a-a-l-ly good way for women to communicate. She wears tight black slogan T-Shirts and jeans or ultra-short metallic-coloured skirts. 'Although I'm a feminist, I should have the right to wear whatever I choose', she tells men in Usenet discussion groups. Her favourite boots would have got her thrown out of the army for wearing unnecessarily aggressive footwear.

Thanks to two cyberfeminist friends, grrrrl@cs.vancouver.edu and sappho@xs4all.ne, she began campaigning against pornography on the Net. This led to her e-mail account being inundated with photographs of women in varying states of undress, which in turn led her to enable the 'bozo-filter' function on her college e-mail software.

She sends vitriolic protest e-mails to President Chirac after getting his address from an activists' mailing list – and receives an automatically generated reply thanking her for her interest and suggesting she visit the French government's home page. She goes on protest rallies with a battered laptop covered in

Friends of the Earth stickers and a mobile phone so that she can e-mail the rally slogans direct to the college computer.

She recently had a crisis when her aquarium full of pond life fell over and spilled tadpoles into her keyboard. This was doubly disastrous because it meant her modem wasn't working so she couldn't post a 'Help! Need advice on getting seaweed out of floppy disk drive' message on Usenet.

She hangs around second-hand record stores looking for CDs of Amazonian rainforest sounds to upload onto the Internet. She spends a lot of time listening to RealAudio whale music she has downloaded.

Hettie wears big cardigans, leggings and Doc Martens made of cruelty-free leather substitute.

She'd like to spray pro-environmentalist slogans on walls, but since she discovered that spray paint contains CFCs she has had to make do with posting stuff on the Net instead.

The Cyberpunk

TOP TEN WAYS TO TELL A...
CYBERPUNK

10. Says things like 'There's this great band in San Francisco. I only heard 15 seconds of their latest single before the hard disk crashed'
9. Has a notebook with lists of 'phree' fone-card numbers
8. Wears mirror shades and trainers
7. Swaps stolen computer passwords with his friends
6. Always looking in the garbage cans outside big companies
5. Has a very complex home telephone set-up connected to his computer
4. Gives out an 800 number on his business card
3. Doesn't trust anyone over thirty
2. Calls a pencil a 'carbide graffiti tool'
1. Publishes free Microsoft software on the Internet for download

What marks out the Cyberpunks is often rock star-style good looks, youth and a complete, jargon-studded sub-culture of clothes, music, gadgets and card numbers. Long hair is still in

ALL DAY'S

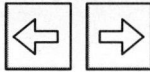

with this gang, and so are short hair, blue hair, mohicans, goths and skin. When people say the 90s are going to make the 60s look like the 50s, it is in Malcolm and his friends that their hopes reside.

Known by his Net-name of 'The Cardinal', Malcolm likes a lot of sex, often accompanied by smart drugs – harmless organic compounds that he believes increase the flow of oxygen to the brain. But he has yet to meet a girlfriend who can talk about computers. There are almost no female Cyberpunks (although there are many Cybergroupies (see below)). The last time Malcolm trusted a female Cyberpunk he was badly let down. She sold her story to *Dot Not*.

The magazine devoted an entire issue to his ex's exposés of everything from lockpicking to computer-cracking. He missed her. She could stay up all night writing UNIX source code and still be ready for a shag at 7am the next morning. But looking back on it, right from the start she had been in it for the kudos, and she had mercilessly exploited her cyberpunk connections to get it. Flame777 was her handle – and, boy, could she flame with the best of them! Now she was making a Channel 4 documentary about… guess what.

Not that The Cardinal is too bothered. He is more worried about getting his own personal 800 number and about the latest Pulp single.

The Geek

TOP TEN WAYS TO TELL A...
GEEK

10. First computer was an Amiga
9.   Learnt to program in Basic while still at school
8.   Spends a lot of time on MUDs
7.   Superior, I-know-best attitude
6.   Has a pocket full of floppy disks
5.   Carries a Newton
4.   Pops over to the computer lab in the lunch break
3.   Spotty from years staring at the screen
2.   Spends hours downloading files from the Internet on the basis they might be useful
1.   Say things like 'I get 160 e-mail messages a day'

Howard works for a University computing department in California. His vital role – building the Net. His job is to forever widen and deepen the global links between computers.

Howard was very annoyed when the 'grunge' look came in because this meant that he was at the forefront of youth fashion for the first time in his life. He hasn't been through a sixties phase yet, not even in the sixties.

He has a text-only account, which he persists in using via the cumbersome command-line interface even though there are hundreds of nice graphical front-ends available. He gets nostalgic about the Old Days when he talked to people on Fidonet and felt that this was being really subversive. He still runs a BBS, but nobody logs on any more because all the files there are for the Spectrum.

The Netropolitan

TOP TEN WAYS TO TELL A...
NETROPOLITAN

10. Says things like 'It's so much easier to send an e-mail than hop on a plane'

9. Keeps a laptop in his golf-bag

8. Books his airline tickets via the Internet

7. Has an e-mail address in somewhere like Bermuda or the Dutch Antilles

6. Reads the *Electronic Telegraph* every day

5. Has a GSN satellite dish on the roof of his Range Rover

4. Has an account with Sharelink

3. Has the Internet installed in his mother's nursing home in Bognor Regis so he can visit her via CU-SeeMe

2. Has a virtual company with offices in three capital cities and no staff

1. Buys a new computer every six months

CHARLES THE NETROPOLITAN

His favourite gizmo is his Powermac portable, which he bought in Hong Kong for a few hundred dollars. He has it connected to his GSN cellphone, which is great for London and New York but not much else. He is forever deciding his travel routing by reference to whether his phone will work while he is travelling. He has about 25 phones in his ten-room 'main home' in Bermuda, but this not always enough and he checks the phones in Duty Free whenever he goes through an airport in case he can find a new model or some extra feature that none of his existing phones can boast. His favourite is the cordless speakerphone, which means he can lie on the beach and talk to London while reading the *Financial Times*. He has a trust fund but dabbles in import/export. Although he lives in Bermuda, he spends more time in his Kensington flat, a large three-bed studio. Occasionally he goes to Royal Garden Parties.

He hangs out at Tramp, where he is trying to persuade the owner to get on the Net and take bookings by e-mail. He is also

Bytes
>>>PRINCE CHARLES ON THE NET

The Prince of Wales took to the Internet today, almost exactly 20 years after his mother became the first Head of State to use the global computer network.

Prince Charles was making his debut on the info-highway with the text of a speech urging the development of a new business ethic. His mother made an unexpected return when a London Internet company broadcast her 1994 Christmas speech via the Internet Mbone — the multimedia part of the Internet.

hoping to save money on phone calls by phoning his girlfriends while they are at the club and speaking to them via the Internet.

His best e-mail friend is his broker, who sits for 12 hours a day surrounded by four screens: Bloomberg, Reuters, Telerate and the Internet.

FAVOURITE NETROPOLITAN WEB SITES

http://www.skyguy.com/~baron/
The exotic aircraft company builds, flies and maintains vintage aircraft from this site. And if you survive crashing your plane they'll come along and sort that out as well.
baron@skyguy.com.

Other favourite sites
http://www.webcom.com/~wta/center.html

http://www.casinomagic.com/

Magic begins at the Magic Casino Web site. Listing all their own casinos plus links to casino sites with on-line gambling.

http://yyy.algorithms.com/cmychv.html
The Cape May Harbor and Village Yacht club. This site offers the chance to buy and rent exclusive waterfront houses and yachts in New Jersey. Other links to equally exclusive sites. <colsona@algorithms.com>

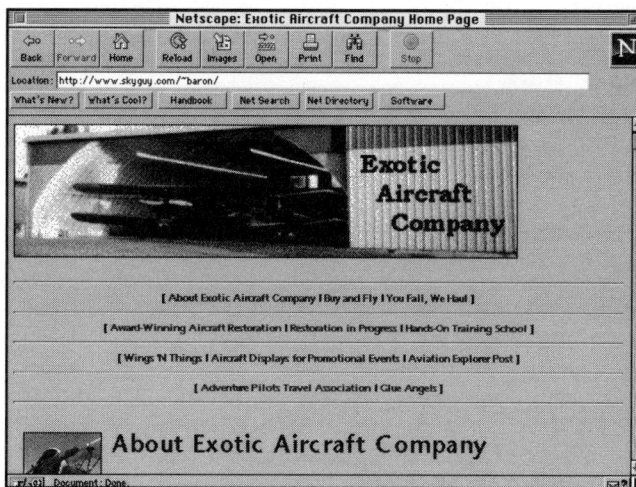

Netscape: Exotic Aircraft Company Home Page

Back Forward Home Reload Images Open Print Find Stop

Location: http://www.skyguy.com/~baron/

What's New? What's Cool? Handbook Net Search Net Directory Software

Exotic Aircraft Company

[About Exotic Aircraft Company I Buy and Fly I You Fail, We Haul]

[Award-Winning Aircraft Restoration I Restoration in Progress I Hands-On Training School]

[Wings 'N Things I Aircraft Displays for Promotional Events I Aviation Explorer Post]

[Adventure Pilots Travel Association I Glue Angels]

About Exotic Aircraft Company

Document: Done.

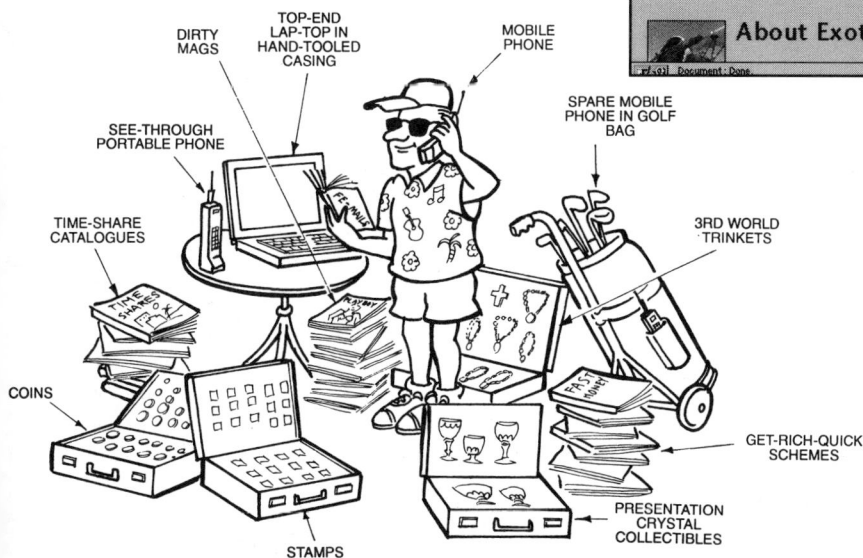

DIRTY MAGS

TOP-END LAP-TOP IN HAND-TOOLED CASING

MOBILE PHONE

SEE-THROUGH PORTABLE PHONE

SPARE MOBILE PHONE IN GOLF BAG

TIME-SHARE CATALOGUES

3RD WORLD TRINKETS

COINS

GET-RICH-QUICK SCHEMES

PRESENTATION CRYSTAL COLLECTIBLES

STAMPS

Chapter

4

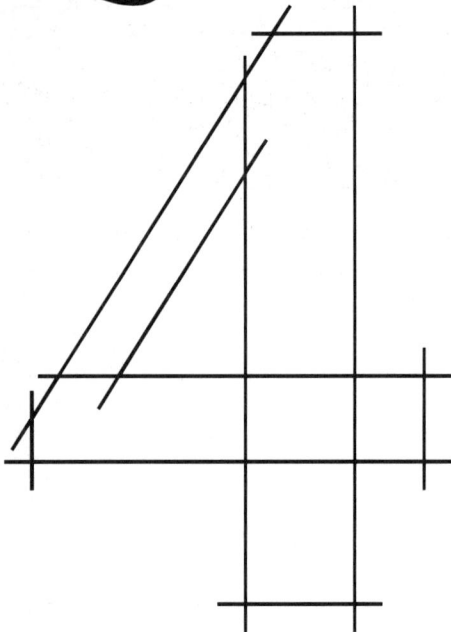

GETTING STARTED

Unlike Mr Newbie, read a book first! Some Internet providers compared: Abel International, Atlas, BBC Networking Club, Pipex, County Internet Services, CompuServe, Cygnet, Delphi, Demon, Electric Mail, Easynet, Hiway, Nethead, Planet Internet

Mr Newbie visits some computer shops – but fails to find what he wants Shops: Best Buys, Morgans, Tempo, Microworld, Shyamtronics, Sony, MicroAnvika, Patel's Electric,

Products: The AST Advantage 812, US Robotics modem, Unisys, Motorola Internet Solution, Minky Mouse coat, gender changers and surge protectors, multimedia cards, compact storage units, Penthouse Interactive CD-ROM, Internet for Dummies, the world's most popular CD-ROM

MR NEWBIE TRIES TO GO ONLINE

Although his only home computer was an ancient Amiga, Mr Newbie had faith that if he could find the right Internet provider everything would work on the silicon-age eqivalent of an antique.

Armed with a copy of *Dot Not*, a magazine aimed at Newbies, he began ringing service providers – the companies that provide the connection between individual consumers and the Internet. He found that there were dozens of companies that have invested in the hardware and the 'user interface' required to provide an Internet service. In all, *Dot Not* listed 117 in the UK; some were offering very localised services – though not in the Basildon area.

While browsing the ads and listings for Internet providers, Mr Newbie was startled to find several advertisements for adult BBs (bulletin boards) and adult Web sites featuring open-mouthed young women with tousled hair giving a 'come sit on it' look – as Mrs Newbie rather coarsely remarked when he showed her the magazine over dinner.

Wondering whether this was really going to be as good for Bert's education as his wife believed, Mr Newbie forged on and started dialing. His first call was to Abel International, where he found a recorded message asking him to leave his details. He hung up. The man who answered the phone at the BBC Networking Club said that they no longer dealt with Internet connections and encouraged Mr Newbie to sign up with another company called Pipex. This struck Mr Newbie as rather strange. Were the BBC supposed to advertise? And wasn't Pipex an American company? The man at the BBC Networking Club said he didn't know. He explained that once the BBC had reached 5,000 members they had achieved what they set out to do and handed their entire subscription base over to Pipex. From now on, it transpired, they would concentrate on building Web pages advertising BBC programmes.

Many of the companies only wanted to mail an information pack and swiftly dealt with any questions by saying 'It's all in the pack.' County Internet Services Ltd. played him an electronic version of Greensleeves for just under seven minutes before saying they no longer dealt with residential connections.

Netscape: NETWELCOME SAYS WELCOME NEWBIE!

http://www.netwelcome.com/index.html

NetWelcome Says, "Welcome, Newbie!"

sit Our Other Sites

Mr Newbie stopped and made a cup of tea. It was 11.30 and he had not yet left first base. He decided to start back at the As again. He called Aladdin, who certainly tried to be helpful but only succeeded in confusing him further. The tech support man told him he would need software called 'winsock'. Surely, he thought, that's something you get at airports to tell whether a plane is likely to crash on its final descent. Mr Newbie wrote WINDSOCK in big letters in the margin of the *Dot Not* page he was using. He also learnt that a modem is a box that connects a computer to a telephone socket, allowing you to dial up to the Internet. He brightened up considerably when Atlas said they could offer him a free home page, but his interest waned when they added that they would take it down after a few weeks 'if it's no good…'. Charming!

The Atlas people were friendly but did not have a very good sales pitch. No attempt was made to sway Mr Newbie to their cause. After two hours of hard sell he felt almost disappointed.

The salesperson at BOGOMIP sounded a little confused himself, which did not put Mr Newbie at ease. He ploughed on, asking whether BOGOMIP could sell him a modem – only to be told he could get a better, cheaper modem elsewhere. What a chump! The trick is to sell to customers, not slag off your own stock, thought Mr Newbie, and he briefly considered going into the Internet business until he realised that he knew nothing about what was obviously already a crowded market.

He called BT and was plunged into an electronic maze of digital questions and push-button telephone answers. After speaking to three different people he discovered that BT was still testing residential connections but that he could expect them to be available 'very soon'. They even offered to call him back when a date was announced. 'I might have dropped off my twig by then', he thought darkly.

CompuServe were very charming and informative. A cheerful girl told Mr Newbie he could even shop at Selfridges via the Net. This was interesting. He had been to Selfridges. The package they offered sounded pretty complicated – the first month was free, then you paid £6.50 per month (though that would change shortly, he was told) with a free 5 hours each month and subsequent hours costing £1.50. This was more than most of the outfits he had spoken to that morning, but they explained that he would get greater reliability, the knowledge that wherever he was in the world there would always be a 'local node', and CompuServe's proprietary software, which sounded very good. News, hobbies, discussion groups were all included, as well as access to the World Wide Web (WWW).

Mr Newbie said he would call back later. He continued his research. Cygnet and Delphi were very helpful, but the man from Delphi admitted that the service did not have graphics. Another salesman talking down his product! Mr Newbie was unimpressed, but not as unimpressed as he would have been had he signed up before discovering the lack of graphics software on Delphi.

Electric Mail were very enthusiastic until they discovered they were dealing with a personal caller. Then they said curtly 'Try Demon' and hung up.

Demon – apparently the biggest of the consumer Internet providers – was always busy. He never did get through. Oh well.

Easynet were a little abrupt and seemingly begrudged answering the phone. Hiway were reassuring. The salesman understood instantly that he was dealing with an ignoramus but did not think the worse of him for it. When Mr Newbie mentioned his worries about his son seeing the adult content they were genuinely concerned. Apparently they 'sit on an Internet backbone', which sounded very uncomfortable. At Nethead Limited in South London, they certainly have their act together. They said "Sales or Service?" as soon as they answered the phone.

"You've come to the right place", Sean in Sales told Mr Newbie after he was put through. Sean said Nethead would send him all the software he needed to get connected for £25 and £7.50 a month.

Planet Internet had an 0800 number and very helpful sales staff. Mr Newbie almost gave them his credit card number on the spot. But by this time his head was spinning from the variety of competing offers and he was worrying about his phone bill – both the one he had run up that morning and the potential bill from the local calls he would make once he was hooked up to the Net. He paused to consider his position.

MR NEWBIE PERSEVERES

Mr Newbie had had enough of dialing-finger fatigue. It was time to take to the streets for some advice. Tottenham Court Road, London – the best place for computer shops in the UK – was where he chose to cruise.

He started off in New Oxford Street, checking out a place called 'Best Buys' first. He walked in and made his way through the smoky haze – it looked like a card game was going on at the back. As he was the only person in the shop he was seen to straight away. They were not very helpful and only had 14.4kbps (kilobytes per second) modems in stock. Newbie had seen the advice in *Internut* (*sic*) magazine – buy a 28.8kbps modem as it sucks down the information twice as fast. Even better, buy an ISDN phone line (£400 installation fee) and a £1,000 Cisco router and you have ten times the speed.

His head spinning, Newbie crossed the road to Morgans, which was filled with customers – some irate because they had been there so long. He waited for about ten minutes before being seen by a nice young man, who apologised that they did not sell modems and recommended two computers instead.

Mr Newbie walked back towards Tottenham Court Road and popped into Tempo. The assistant seemed shocked when Mr Newbie told him he wanted to get connected to the Internet but had no computer. Nevertheless, he was very friendly and explained everything using easy-to-understand terms. He recommended an AST Advantage 812 that had a 28.8kbps US Robotics modem and 8 megabytes of RAM. The price was a snip at £1699! The package included connection to the Internet and Windows 3.11.

Microworld, also in Tottenham Court Road, had more of a bazaar atmosphere. There seemed to be a lot of staff, but he still had to wait ten minutes before being greeted by a chirpy African man wearing a snakeskin sweatshirt. 'Relax,' said the man, 'take a seat! You've been waiting for long enough!' He was very helpful and keen to bargain, offering to knock the price down before Mr Newbie had said a word. He talked Newbie through all the features in their multimedia package. He reckoned that everything (including Net connection) would come to £1,500. Not bad.

Just up the road, Shyamtronics had only one computer system on offer – Unisys. As he walked out of the shop the assistant called after him 'Don't you want to take it now? Can't we do a deal for you?' Newbie didn't look back.

He stepped into the Sony Shop and was confronted by an eager sales assistant. Too eager. She stood uncomfortably close to him and obviously thought that flirting was a sure-fire way to get a sale. Wrong. They didn't sell personal computers anyway and only offered him the Motorola Internet Solution software package for £249. A few doors down, at MicroAnvika, the same package was £195. They were very busy and Newbie had to wait. He tried to bargain with the assistant but had no luck.

Seeing all the kit on display prompted him to wonder what he needed besides the basic computer and keyboard – whether there was something that would make his computer life more complete.

First up, he spotted some 'Scream Beat' speakers. Did that mean that son Bert could download heavy rock without fear of his speakers bursting? Across the aisle were Sound Blaster cards. Maybe he could use one to create his own Internet disco. But his favourite item was the 'Minky Mouse Coat' – a pink, fluffy cover to place over one's mouse. And the Looney Tunes mouse mat featuring Taz would definitely add a bit of colour to his desk. Why have boring grey when you could have a Tasmanian Daredevil?

Sitting in a rack next to the Minky Mouse covers were some grey tubes called 'Gender Changers'. Could it be true? Had technology moved so fast that he could now change sex by plugging himself into his computer? The small print said: 'The practical way to change the gender of your cable connectors or peripherals'. The equally suggestively named Surge Protectors turned out to protect your computer against sudden changes in

voltage. Cables were well taken care of – you could buy them their own ties (to keep them neat) in a range of colours. Clearly, if you knew what sex your cable was you could choose pink or blue accordingly.

The Win/TV Celebrity Multimedia card offered 'frame grabbing on the fly'. This made Newbie think of 70s 'Shaft'-style street slang: 'So, Tony, where you been? You get the stuff?' 'Cool it man, I've been frame grabbing on the fly.' The Homestyle compact storage units were a good idea in principle, but in practice they were just beige chipboard cupboards. You won't find those in my home, thought Newbie.

It is billed as 'Be a Penthouse Photographer'. The aim of the game is to graduate from the Penthouse photography school. Watch some video clips of all-American girls at play. Maybe choose a blonde today. Dress her in a cheerleader's pom-pom, perhaps, and not much else? Then the moment of artistic decision – whether to take the snap while she has the baseball bat between her breasts or wait till she puts it between her legs. Hey, let's go for both. Set the aperture and the exposure or select 'Automatic'. The preloaded video clips last a few minutes each.

Once the virtual 'shoot' is over it only remains to take the film back to the 'labs' and work on it a bit more, then deliver the finished set of contacts to *Penthouse* magazine.

The game ends with *Penthouse* publisher Bob Guccione appearing on screen to appraise the work and offer you a job.

Penthouse Interactive from ICFX Inc.
POB 955 Fairfax CA 9491 Tel. 415 485 5850

The world's most **popular**

CD ROM

He liked the look of the software packages. They even had Internet for Dummies. But it was too complicated. 'Do I need a dummy guide to the Internet guide for Dummies too?' Mr Newbie wondered desperately as he moved next door to Patel's Electric, which appeared to be completely unattended. Two children were playing a filthy CD ROM game on a computer at the back. Mr Newbie was appalled.

NORBERT THE NET-VET RESCUES MR NEWBIE FROM COMPUTER HELL

Glad that on this occasion he was not with his son, Mr Newbie struck up a conversation with Norbert, who had popped in to buy an ethernet card while up in London visiting his auntie. With Norbert's assistance Mr Newbie bought a 486 PC with speakers, a built-in modem and no CD-ROM drive. 'If you've got a modem you don't really need a CD-ROM drive,' Norbert told him. 'CD-ROMs are used to distribute big files – bigger than can fit on a floppy disk. But you can download files over the phone via your modem.' Mr Newbie did not understood the logic of this, and Norbert had to leave before Newbie could ask him to recommend the right Internet provider.

He sat in a taxi with his new computer. As they sped towards Basildon Mr Newbie saw a PC World flash by. He made the driver turn round and sprinted inside to buy the first Internet package he could find. Big mistake. He came back with Net-

in-the-Box, a book and disk set, which promised that its easy-install software would allow you to get straight on the Net.

Mr Newbie had become a man obsessed. Nothing would stop him becoming the first on his street with access to the Net. He would be a Net-pioneer, following in the footsteps of… well, who exactly? Where did the Net come from? Had the earliest Internet users had the same problems of difficult Internet providers and questionable hardware?

Chapter

5

THE NET PIONEERS

Charles Babbage and Lady
Ada Lovelace

The three ages of computers
and the birth of IBM

The scientists who built
the Net

Tim Berners-Lee – inventor
of the Web

Bill Gates – the biggest
Net-head of all

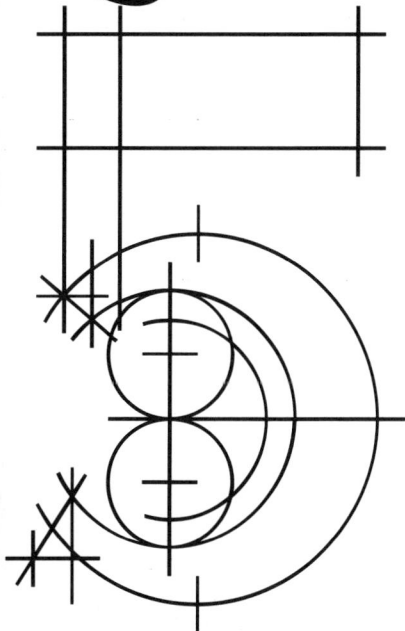

The earliest prototype Net-head was Charles Babbage (1791-1871). If he was alive today, Babbage would have his own e-mail address. The BBC have even named their Web site after him. He invented the first computer, which he called an 'analytical engine', in 1842. It was literally the first home computer – Babbage built it in a workshop at the back of his Marble Arch house in London. The machine combined a miniature version of Robert Louis Stevenson's steam engine with a system of gears and shafts.

Babbage's mistress, Ada Lady Lovelace, daughter of Lord Byron, was also an archetypal Net-head. She even wrote some simple computer programmes. She tried to use the analytical engine to develop an infallible gambling system – and ran up huge gambling debts as a result.

Lady Lovelace was also one of the first to speculate on whether machines could actually think. She realised that basically computers are very stupid and, although they may seem clever, in fact they can only do exactly what they are told: 'The Analytical engine has no pretensions whatever to originate anything,' she wrote to a friend. 'It can do whatever we know how to order it to perform. It can follow analysis; but it has no powers of anticipating any analytical relationships or truths. Its province is to assist us in making available what we are already acquainted with.'

Babbage was the role model for future Geeks. He wanted to create a geek-only club, called the Royal Society, which is now Britain's premiere scientific establishment. His crowning achievement was his contemptuous treatment of the feckless aristocrats who were joining the Society in the early 19th century. Scorning social preferment, Babbage wanted to dump the aristos and restrict membership to genuine scientists. After a bitter campaign he succeeded.

The next giant of the computer age was the first in a long line of American techno-nerds: Herman Hollerith built a 'tabulating machine' to compile the results of the 1890 US census. The 1880 census results had taken seven years to complete. Hollerith's machine completed the 1890 results in just three years.

He then founded the Tabulating Machine Company. In 1924 the name was changed to International Business Machines Corporation, or IBM. The IBM global network is now the most far-flung and advanced private network in the world.

In the 1940s, as other companies sprang up to compete, IBM hired Howard Aiken to build a general-purpose computer which could perform any task given to it. The result was the Automatic Controlled Sequence Calculator, which was 40 feet long by 10 feet high. It had about the same computing power as a low-priced solar-powered calculator that a schoolchild might use today.

THE THREE AGES OF COMPUTERS

1. The Black-Box Age (1939-70)
Computers were a giant mass of vacuum tubes, transistors or integrated circuits. They filled a warehouse. If you smoked or raised your voice they wheezed to a halt. Most of them were made by IBM.

2. The Personal Assistant Age (1970-90)
The invention of microchips and new operating systems meant that smaller, cheaper computers could do bigger jobs faster. Micro-miniaturisation and better software put computers within reach of small businesses and homes. By the end of the Personal Assistant Age most people had switched to software produced by Microsoft.

3. The Network Age (1992-?)
The Internet was started in 1970 by the defence industry and academic researchers working on a prototype indestructible global computer communications network. A few dozen researchers at seven sites in the US, the UK and Norway were the sum total of all Net-heads. This new communications medium caught on because the operators started sending each other messages to share research ideas and discuss common interests. That was the birth of e-mail.

Twenty years later there were hundreds of thousands of Net-heads – all still academics and computer professionals, and mostly men. But the invention of the World Wide Web, launched in 1993, attracted millions to join them.

WHO ACTUALLY INVENTED
THE INTERNET?

Professor Nicholas Negroponte, head of the New Media Lab at MIT is one of the most revered thinkers of the digital age. He thinks that Dr Larry Roberts is the great forgotten genius who invented the Internet. But Negroponte is out of touch. It was not Roberts. The Internet was 'invented' in concept in 1979 by Paul Baran, Vint Cerf, Jon Postel and Bob Braden, now Executive Director of the Internet Architecture Board.

Some thirty years ago the RAND Corporation, America's foremost Cold War think-tank, faced a strange strategic problem. How could the US Army successfully communicate in the event of a nuclear war? They needed a way of routing around war zones so that a message would reach its destination. The Internet turned out to be the answer. Each message is split up into small packets of data and is sent out on the computer network. It goes to its destination by whatever route is available, passing through many other computers on the way, each of them part of the global network. At the final destination the receiving computer assembles the message. If one of the packets is missing, the receiving computer sends a message to the sending computer asking it to send the missing packet again.

Paul Baran worked at the RAND corporation at that time, running the project. The project was called DARPanet (Defense Advanced Research Project Network). He now heads Com 21 Inc., an Internet phone company offering voice, data and video services.

Vint Cerf is commonly known as the Father of the Internet. Cerf invented the computer protocols used in DARPanet and its successor, ARPANet, to allow different kinds of computers to speak to each other. He is now senior vice president for data architecture at MCI, a US phone company that has formed an alliance with BT and Rupert Murdoch's News Corporation.

Jon Postel is Project Leader of the US National Science Foundation's Routing Arbiter project and of the ARPA-sponsored Gigabit Network Communications Research Project. Both of these projects are so technical they are completely incomprehensible to anyone who does not, like Postel, have B.S. and M.S. degrees in Engineering and a Ph.D. in Computer Science from UCLA. His current interests include multi-machine internetwork applications, multimedia conferencing, electronic mail, very large networks and very high speed communications. Way to go, Jon!

But perhaps the most important figure of all is a young Englishman who single-handedly invented the World Wide Web. Tim Berners-Lee did not participate in the building of the Net itself. But what he did was just as important. He dreamt up the World Wide Web – the 'killer application' of the Internet. The Web is the reason that most people are going onto the Net. Even though still in its infancy, the Web is a fascinating, if badly organised, global library. Once it is fully formed it could be awesome.

Tim Berners-Lee is the man the Net-vets most admire. He invented the World Wide Web in 1989 at CERN, the European Particle Physics Laboratory in Geneva. The Web is what transformed the Net from an academic backwater into the global infotainment arcade it is today.

The Web is simply a way of storing and sharing information via computer networks. When the information is presented there are links within the text or the pictures. It is interactive because, sitting at a computer, you can click on those links and be transported to other, related information, perhaps on the same computer, on the network in the office or on a computer somewhere else in the world.

Software is a young man's game. Berners-Lee created the Web at the relatively old age of 32. At the same age Bill Gates was well on his way to his first billion. Like Gates, Berners-Lee was introduced to computers while still a child. His parents were mathematicians.

After graduating in physics from Oxford University, Berners-Lee developed the first Web prototype in 1980 for his own use. He had the idea fom reading a book written in 1858, *Inquire Within: Anything You Want To Know*, which styled itself as a compendium of all known facts. Eventually Berners-Lee expects the Web to become a place where one can find out any fact about anything in the world, quickly and cheaply.

'I thought that if I could get out a piece of software that is sufficiently fun to use, so that everybody would, in fact, use it for putting down everything they were doing, then the resulting sea of information would allow everything to run much more easily.'

By the time the Web arrived the Internet was already a vast, disorganised swamp of information. Its big advantage was that it was free. But the fascinating work that existed on some computers was obscured by millions of megabytes of out-of-date or just plain boring information on others.

The Web allowed Net-heads to use the internet in a logical way. It created a standard that everybody could – and did – follow.

For Berners-Lee fans, here are the references:

```
http://www.w3.org/hypertext/WWW/People/Berne
rs-Lee/FAQ.html
```

```
http://www.w3.org/hypertext/WWW/People/Berne
rs-Lee-Bio.html
```

```
http://www.sld.slac.stanford.edu/sldwww/beam
line/history.html
```

```
http://www.w3.org/hypertext/Conferences/Over
view-WWW.html
```

```
http://www.w3.org./hypertext/WWW/Talks/Gener
al/Directions.html
```

```
http://www.w3.org./hypertext/WWW/Talks/Gener
al/Protocols.html
```

```
http://www.w3.org/hypertext/WWW/Proposal -
Original proposal at CERN for WWW
```

Berners-Lee, Tim and Robert Caillian, Ari Luotonene, Henrik Frystyk Nielso and Arthur Secret, 'The World Wide Web', *Communications of the ACM,* August 1994, p.76ff.

WHERE DO YOU WANT TO GO TODAY, BILL GATES?

The king of the Net-heads may still turn out to be William H. (Bill) Gates, Chairman and CEO of the Microsoft Corporation. Gates made his $10 billion plus fortune in the pre-network age selling software for indivdual PCs.

Gates is the Net-head all the Profiteers are trying to emulate. From nought to ten billion dollars in 20 years – if anyone can control the anarchic Internet, it ought to be Gates, who founded Microsoft while still a student. The kids who started the early Internet companies like Netscape and Yahoo aren't interested in control, and Rupert Murdoch is not capable of it. Only Gates thinks big enough and retains a childlike lack of self-doubt that could allow him to try and conquer Cyberspace.

The Microsoft Corporation is the world's biggest provider of software for personal computers. Eighty per cent of the world's computers use Bill Gates' software – Windows 95 and Microsoft Office and Microsoft everything else. With an income of $5.94 billion in 1995, Microsoft employs more than 18,000 people in 48 countries. Hundreds of Microsoft millionaires and three billionaires were spawned by the company's meteoric growth. But they were not all whizz-bang programmers. Many of the millionaires were cleaners and clerical workers who happened to take stock options.

Gates' own behaviour makes their task easier. When *Time* magazine asked him about unfair practices by Microsoft, he threw a tantrum. 'I challenge your facts!' he shouted when confronted with an allegation that a Microsoft spokesman confirmed a few days later. 'That's a lie! I mean, it's just not true. I never heard of any such thing. What a bunch of nonsense!' Asked a similar question during a live CBS TV interview with Connie Chung, Gates walked out, saying he didn't have to 'put up with this.'

But the clouds are gathering for Microsoft. Its hugely successful software packages have turned into 'bloatware' – overlarge and ridiculously slow to operate.

Gates began his career in personal computer software at age 13, when he started programming

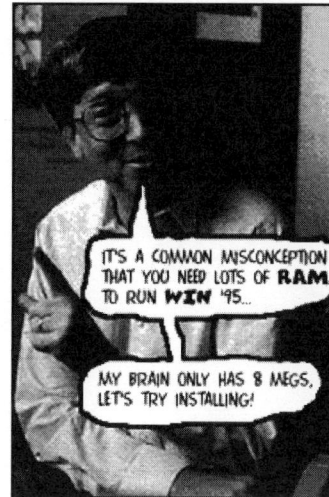

Start Me... Uuuughh!

http://www.king.net/gilmore/head/gates1.html

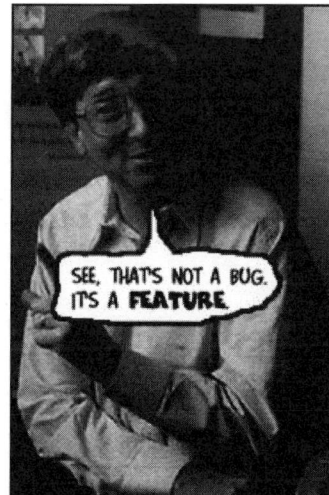

The TOP SIX ways things would be different if
MICROSOFT
built cars...

No.6. A particular model year of car wouldn't be available until AFTER that year, instead of before.

No.5. Occasionally your car would just die for no reason and you'd have to restart it. For some strange reason you would accept this as normal.

No.4. Sun Motorsystems would make a car that was solar-powered, twice as reliable and five times as fast but only ran on 5% of the roads.

No.3. The oil, alternator, petrol and engine warning lights would be replaced by a single 'General Fault' warning light. When it lit up you would have to go straight to the nearest repair shop to get the car fixed.

No.2. People would get excited about the 'new' features in Microsoft cars, forgetting completely that they had been available in other brands for years.

No.1. New seats will force everyone to have the same size ass.

http://www.pe.net/~rthomas/microcars.html

as a hobby. He formed Microsoft with Paul Allen in 1975 to develop software for personal computers. The two had a vision that the PC would soon be on every office desktop and in every home.

Paul Allen is the opposite personality-type to Gates. A sports maniac and showman, Allen likes to be seen on his 150 ft, state-of-the-art white mega-yacht. Bill has no corporate jets. Apart from a short hop to the nearest airport, it's commercial flights only for all Microserfs.

When Gates attended his own 40th birthday party in 1995, he had reached a strange turning point in his life. Just recently listed as the second richest man in America, his company simultaneously seemed more vulnerable to competitors than ever before. Bill's world-beating software might become obsolete when we all use the Internet – and he knows it.

At a meeting of his top staff in April 1994, Gates admitted that Internet 'mania', as he called it, had taken him by surprise. Millions of people were communicating via software standards and application programs over which Microsoft had no control. Gates could even foresee a day when Microsoft's software would be cut out because it didn't work well on the Internet.

Gates' blind spot for the Internet is strange considering he has used it for years to keep control of his vast empire. 'A significant portion of his day is [spent] staying in contact with Microsoft's employees around the world through e-mail' says his official biography on the Microsoft Web site.

The Microsoft Network, originally intended as a pay-as-you-go online service, was redesigned to embrace the Internet. Eventually Microsoft would 'take a little slice out of each transaction', an executive said

To hedge his bets and spread his risk, Gates has also invested in a series of grand alliances – including one with Hollywood's DreamWorks troika (Stephen Spielberg, Jeffrey Katzenberg and Dave Geffen) to make interactive entertainment products. Gates certainly had his photo taken with a lot of famous people as a result of that deal, but he has no idea whether it will make him any money.

He has a $40 million house on the shores of Lake Washington near Seattle that was designed after he married his wife, who he met when she was a secretary at Microsoft. The house has an outer shell and an inner sanctum. The private living quarters are joined to the outer sanctum, but most visitors see only the conference rooms, entertainment rooms and bedrooms in the outer zone.

On the Web you can get photos of the property taken by anti-Bill fanatics who want to deny the billionaire the thing he most prizes. Bill is a very private guy. There are dozens of Net-heads whose whole existence is based around their opposition to Gates. In Usenet newsgroups like 'alt.destroy.microsoft' the Gates-haters come together to lambast the company and its products.

One day Gates might just disappear into Howard Hughes-style seclusion. Right now he is in-your-face, making personal appearances and writing newspaper columns worldwide to boost his stock price.

'He is very, very rich,' said *Time* magazine, 'and so powerful that even his enemies are eager to cut deals with him. Now he wants more, a piece of all the action – the bills people pay, the phone calls they make, the news they read, the TV they watch. But he may have reached that point in the arc of his success where the very qualities that raised him high could start to drag him down.'

Chapter

6

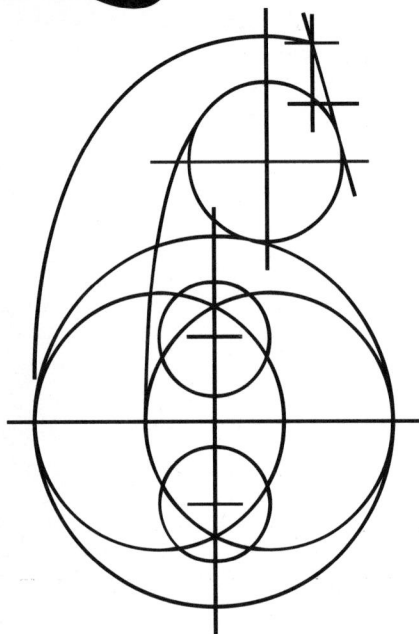

SHOPPING AROUND

Bert takes his dad for a multimedia ride
CyberAddicts
PC World – the perils of tecchie salesmen
CD-ROMs and CD drives
SurfWatch
Dadnet
Installing
Software
Failure

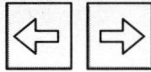

Bert hated shopping for computers with his dad. It was always so embarrassing when Dad started trying to talk about computers. As he sat buckled up in the front passenger seat, Bert was dealing with the situation the only way he knew how. Dad may think he is driving the car to the computer shop, but in fact Bert is driving, using his Super-Nintendo joystick with add-on infra-red capabilities

Bert has seen a physiotherapist about his overdeveloped right hand. But she said it was perfectly normal in the computer age and nothing to worry about. She suggested a double joystick so he could exercise his left hand as well. And for a while Bert had seriously considered it. 'Naw, that's a soppy idea,' he had concluded, 'I need my left hand free for the keypad.' When his best friend John took part in Dr Beelsby's research at the clinic, he clocked up 14 hours a day on the Internet and was declared an addict at a press conference. And John was on the computer far less than Bert. John got on to a Channel 4 documentary as a result, which was really unfair…

Bert suddenly threw his joystick to the left. 'That's it Dad, do a left.… straighten out… ease back and park there. Great!'

IT'S A WARNING LETTER FROM THE SCHOOL…OVERDEVELOPED RIGHT HAND, BULGING STARING EYES, LETHARGIC…HE'S ADDICTED !

Mr Newbie gave his son a strange look but remained silent.

Maybe this wasn't going to be so bad after all, Bert thought, as the pair walked across the car park to the entrance of PC World. Bert examined the four bikers leaving the store, each carrying a CD-ROM drive. CD-ROM? They must be crazy. Yesterday a boy at school said he had managed to call up pictures of Ryan Giggs on an Internet-enabled computer at Escom.

'Dad – can we try out the laptops?' he whined. But Mr. Newbie marched firmly towards the CD-ROM counter as a sales assistant turned expectantly towards him. 'The last time I was here…' he began. But at the mention of the words 'the last time' the assistant turned to the man next to him – who was ready to make a purchase – and began completing his order.

The last time he was there Mr Newbie had bought Net-in-the-Box, 'Your plug and play Net connection.' At home he found to his fury that the software was on a CD-ROM, not on floppy disks. He had a floppy disk drive but no CD-ROM drive, so he had either to exchange the CD-ROM version for the floppy or buy a CD-ROM drive.

The first option was quickly ruled out. 'There is no floppy version, sir' said the assistant. 'There's 450 megabytes of software on that disk. You'd need a shopping trolley to carry it if we gave it to you on floppies.'
'You didn't tell me it was CD-ROM when I bought it', whined Newbie.

Bert cringed at this exchange and looked round the room.

A little black boy at a nearby terminal was being shown how to use Sim City by his father – who obviously did know what he was talking about. Sim City is probably the world's most successful computer simulation game, teaching the young how politicians balance growth against pollution and bribe the voters by building a new football stadium just before an election

'It says "CD-ROM version" on the side, sir.' The sales assistant had adopted a nasty tone of voice. 'Well, how much is a CD-ROM caddie then?' asked Mr Newbie miserably. 'A caddie, sir, is the container you place your disk in in order to play it. What you need is a CD-ROM player, which is a special this week at £295.'

'Its plug and play sir,' he added, while Mr Newbie paused in a misery of indecision.
'I bet' thought Bert, who had spent the previous night trying to install a plug and play sound card. He had finally been allowed to go to bed at three in the morning.

'OK,' said Mr Newbie, 'I suppose we'd better get the quad speed.'
'Thank you sir' said the assistant. 'Of course, with the quad speed you'll need an extra 4Mb of RAM to get the full effect. It's on special this week sir – only £99.'

Bert brightened up. He had been begging his dad for an extra 4Mb of RAM, the active memory on a computer that determines how fast the software will run. He wanted it to play Doom. Now he would be able to play network Doom with his friend Jason as soon as Jason's dad figured out how to install the modem software.

Bytes

CYBERADDICTS

According to some estimates, 2-3% of the online community have a serious 'Internet addiction' and spend most of their waking time surfing and chatting. But John Robards of the Boston Computer Society says 'Give me a break. We're not talking about alcohol or drug abuse. I understand people are mentally weak and can form a so-called addiction, but at the same time, people are making an excuse for not having a life.'

http://www.bcs.org/bcs/

With the CD-ROM drive sorted, it was time to turn to other pressing matters. 'Do you have CyberSitter, Net Nanny or SurfWatch, please?' asked Mr Newbie. Bert woke from his reverie at the sound of SurfWatch. He hadn't heard of them, but they sounded bad, *really* bad. Was this the beginning of some parental attempt to control his access?

'I don't think so' Bert whispered to himself, mimicking his favourite star, Beavis from MTV. He craned his neck anxiously over the counter as the assistant began explaining the relative merits of SurfWatch and Net Nanny.

'They are all designed to be multi-functional,' began the salesman. 'You can use them to restrict your children's access at home and the staff access at work.

'Inter-Censor and SurfWatch are similar in that you cannot tamper with the list of banned sites. The Inter-Censor bannings are decided by a minister of the Mormon church in Utah. He uploads them to the central server, and the latest additions to the banned site list are automatically loaded to your hard disk the moment you next log on.

'If you try to tamper with it, the software sends a warning back to Utah, your hard drive is immediately disabled and you will be contacted within seven days by a minister of a non-denominational Church in your local area.'

'Well, that all sounds perfectly reasonable…' began Mr Newbie.

But the salesman had not yet finished his patter. 'The minister is assisted by a hand-picked team of Moral Majority scrutineers from around the world. Not one of them is under 50.

'The entire service is yours for £149.99, with nothing more to pay for the first six months. After that the updates are £70 a month, including a free CD of the Greatest Gospel Music Hits by Billy Joe and the Gunslingers.'

The salesman produced a newspaper article about the product by Wavey K. Kramer, but Mr Newbie had lost interest at the mention of the price. And he didn't think much of Wavey Kramer, who seemed to endorse products produced by his masters at Web Corp.

'There ought to be something free for kids', he couldn't help saying. And to his surprise the salesman agreed. 'Try DadNet' he advised. 'Its a very low-profile organisation in Scandinavia, and its not listed in any of the search engines. But they do have access to software that will help one-parent families enable their children to use the Net while the dad is cooking dinner.'

Mr Newbie blanched at the thought of ever having to control even one child and cook dinner at the same time. He thanked the salesman for his advice, happily paid his bill for £499.98, and agreed to let Bert spend a while looking round the shop on the strict understanding they weren't buying anything.

Half an hour later the pair walked back to the car with an encyclopaedia on CD-ROM and another one about World War 2. Mr Newbie reasoned that this was educational material for Bert, and Granddad might enjoy it when he came to stay next Christmas.

After lunch Mr Newbie and Bert trudged up to the study and, while his father began unpacking the modem, Bert read through the installation instructions for Net-in-the-Box and a CD-ROM guide to the Internet, which Mr Newbie had been given a few weeks previously at the Sky TV/Internet for Very Small Businesses traveling roadshow. The CD-ROM stuff looked pretty simple really. Just rewrite the '.ini' file, create a new '.exe' file, twiddle a few interrupts and away you went!

It was almost midnight by the time the two were able to attempt their first log-on. It turned out that they had achieved the correct settings at 7pm – it was just that the log-on phone number they had been given by Net-in-the-Box had succumbed to the volume of calls at the peakest of peak times and gone U/S for several hours.

Now the two were brought together by that father-and-son bond. They had suffered together and come through together – scarred perhaps – but they had triumphed over the technology. Bert

went wearily to bed, while Mr Newbie stayed up to surf the Net at last.

Unfortunately, without Bert the digitally-challenged Mr Newbie was lost. Only after his son had fallen asleep did he finally admit to himself that without the 12-year-old he was incapable of functioning computer-wise.

Several days later Bert and his father jointly concluded that Net-in-the-Box was just too complicated. Reluctantly Mr Newbie swallowed his pride (and a £50 loss) and switched to BT Online, run by the phone company.

Chapter 7

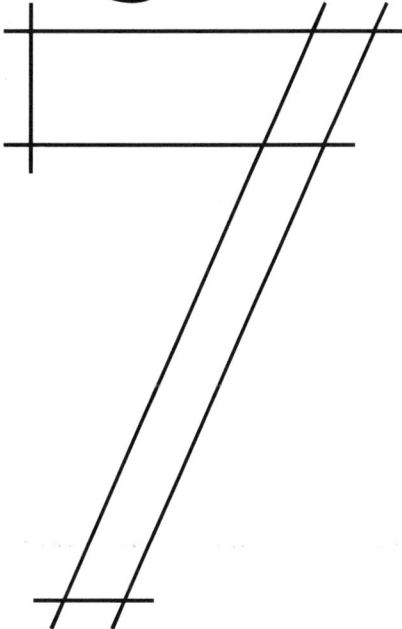

FIRST NET EXPERIENCES

MR NEWBIE'S FIRST NET EXPERIENCE

Mr Newbie arrived back from work on Friday with a very good idea of how he was going to spend the weekend. Junior had been beta-testing the new software all week and now was the time to go surfing. He had certainly paid his dues: 53 days after he had first given the BT Online service his credit card number, and after the nice man in tech support had promised him it would only take a couple of hours even for a complete novice, he was ready to go surfing

Bert set his dad up, made sure he had logged on to the server and headed for bed. Mr Newbie decided the first thing he would try were the so-called 'Newsgroups'.

FONE PHREAKS

There are more than 14,000 newsgroups on the Internet. They are specialist discussion groups where anyone can join in the conversation. They might include learned professors and total stumble-bums who delight in insulting their fellow-participants.

OKAY NOW DAD, WE'RE GOING TO PRACTISE THREE POINT TURNS

They work like a giant electronic noticeboard. Net-heads 'post' a message to a newsgroup, and anyone who accesses that group can then read it. They can reply to the message and become part of a 'thread'. Or they can start their own thread.

Newbie took a quick look at a newsgroup called 'alt.ph.uk'.

```
In article: <4d5rog$ecc@spider.rmplc.co.uk>
donc@rmplc.co.uk (>c=c=o ketene) writes:

> I`m getting phonecalls on my Sony Walkman
(not a wind-up).
> The frequency is set at @1600KHz AM, the
house is about
> 350m away and I can hear both sides of
the conversation.
> What is going on here, is this a mobile
or a cordless I'm hearing?

you're getting cordless phone transmissions.
The handset transmits on 47 or 48 MHz,
paired with the base station tx around
1700kHz. Although you're only monitoring one
side of a 2-freq pair, the base unit
connects to the POTS so you get both sides
of the chat.
```

MY FIRST NEWS GROUP

Interesting, but not very interesting. Reminding himself to return the next time he had weird technical questions, Mr Newbie turned to a group that was tailor-made for him: alt.news.newbies. He cast an eye over some of the more technical-looking topics.

```
'Re: Help!' (4 messages)
'Re: Test' (1 message)
'Re: Help needed (urgent) with modem in San
Francisco' (2 messages)
'Re: Test - please ignore' (3 messages)
'Re: Hlp me plaese somebody' (16 messages)
'Re: AAAAAAAAAAAAAGHH!!!?!' (54 messages)
```

```
'Re: Where do I find all the XXX rated
stuff?' (20 messages)
'Re: just testing' (4 messages)
'Re: ***HOT SEX CALL THIS 0800 NUMBER***'
(87 messages)
'Re: Mating habits of Siamese Fighting Fish'
(2 messages)
'Re: Posting to wrong newsgroup' (10
messages)
```

This seemed to be the place to find the more experienced Net-heads dispensing helpful advice. Advice like 'Get a life you sad person' or 'The new 28.8 made all the difference' repeated eight times and followed by the message: 'Subject: Sorry - new software!!!!! Wasn't sure if you got that.'

Mr Newbie consulted his 'Guide to Netiquette', which he'd carefully ripped out of *Dot-Not* magazine. There are certain rules, it said, which should be observed in order to maintain the respect of the Usenet community.

NETIQUETTE:
MR NEWBIE: DON'T ASK OBVIOUS QUESTIONS

Mr Newbie threw down his copy of Dimwit's Guide To Usenet in frustration. 'I've looked through the index seven times now', he moaned. 'I've read every page at least twice and I still can't find out what RTFM stands for. Someone told me to RTFM before I posted any more newsgroup articles. I can find FTP and WWW and URL, but no RTFM anywhere.'

Norbert summoned up his 'patient' expression and sat Newbie down with a cup of herbal tea. 'RTFM,' he explained, 'stands for "Read The Manual".'

'But…'

'Yes, I know there's one letter too many. Don't worry about that. Just be careful not to go asking too many obvious questions. People who've been on the Internet for a while get very fed up with answering the same things time and time again.'

Norbert clicked idly on his mouse button as he was talking. Another screen full of 'Advice Needed: How Do I Decode Picture File??' queries flashed up. He went on:

'If you're new to a particular newsgroup, don't start posting articles straight away. You'll probably find out that you're asking the same things every other newbie asks. That's where the FAQ comes in.'

Mr Newbie looked slightly alarmed. 'What's the fack?'

'It's a TLA.'

'A …?'

'Three Letter Acronym. Stands for "Frequently Asked Questions". Chances are that's where you'll find the answer you're looking for. Most newsgroups have

their FAQ list posted once a week or so – if you lurk for a few days you'll probably be in luck.'

'Oh,' said Mr Newbie. 'Thanks. That's a big help.' And he went off to post an 'Advice Needed: where is the FAQ for this Newsgroup?' question before Norbert could do anything to stop him.

'…and by the way, Norbert, or BTW as they say on the Net. What does the F in RTFM really mean?'

'How about "Friendly"?' Norbert answered.
MR NEWBIE'S FIRST NEWSGROUP

POSTING

His computer whirred, made a noise like an upset stomach and downloaded some more messages from alt.usenet.newbie.

```
'Re: You a full of sh1T' (10 messages)
'Re: Compuserve w*nkers' (14 messages)
'Re: Confused American - what is a w*nker?'
(57 messages)
```

'Before you post,' advised the *Guide to Netiquette*, 'it is a good idea to "lurk" (see also: Lurkers) for a while to get a feel for the conversation. Posting in haste may annoy other users.'

Having been lurking for a good five minutes he decided it was time to make his first posting. He noticed that somebody in Vancouver had posted a message offering:

```
>Ultimate Guide To The Internet - a must
have for total newbies
```

HEY, IT **IS** RATHER FRIENDLY AFTER ALL!

```
>By Wavey K. Kramer (Webmaster and author
of 'The Complete Dweeb's Guide To Widgets',
'The Complete Widget's Guide To Dweebs',
'The Complete Guide To Net Jargon',
>
Covers Usenet, FTP, Gophers, WWW, Email,
IRC and MUCH MORE!
>
> Also includes new chapter - How To Make
Money From The Internet!
>
>For your copy send $45.00 NOW to the
address below. Or email me
>for a Free Sample Chapter!
```

This was obviously an example of the public-spirited way that Internet veterans made their assistance available to less experienced surfers, and Mr Newbie felt pleased to have become a member of such a supportive community. He noticed that several people had already posted messages requesting this 'Free Sample Chapter'; it sounded like an offer that was too good to pass up. Interestingly, some callous soul appeared to have forged another message from Mr Kramer's e-mail address offering 'GIRLS GIRLS GIRLS - ADULTS ONLY GIFs ON NEW WWW SITE!' He wasn't altogether sure what a 'GIF' was, but it sounded unsavoury.

Mr Newbie decided to lose his Usenet virginity by adding his own voice to the demands for the 'Free Sample Chapter'. That way he wouldn't offend anyone. It gave him a nice warm feeling when he clicked on the Send Now button and his message disappeared into the ether with a cheery 'ping' sound.

```
From: newbie@compuserve.com
Newsgroups: alt.new.new-users
Re: Ultimate Guide To The Internet

>For your copy send $45.00 NOW to the
address below. Or email me
>for a Free Sample Chapter!

Send me one too!
```

Mail B

```
My email address is newbie@compuserve.com

Thanks in advance,

Mr Newbie

(newbie@compuserve.com)
```

That ought to do it. He sat back feeling awfully proud of himself and flipped idly on to the next page of his *Guide to Netiquette*.

'Rule Eleven: Never post "Me Too" messages. This is a waste of bandwidth and annoys other Net-heads. See also related topics: Flaming, Mail Bombing, How To Take Legal Action Against Another Internet User.'

The following day Mr Newbie logged excitedly into his e-mail program to see whether his Free Sample Chapter had arrived. There was certainly something there – something big, too, because it was taking an awfully long time to download. Perhaps that nice, public-spirited Mr Kramer had decided to help a struggling new subscriber by sending him the whole of his *Ultimate Guide to the Internet* and waiving the $45.00 fee.

OMBS

Half an hour later Mr Newbie's modem was still making a strange whining noise – and so was Newbie. He sat and stared blankly at the page headed 'Mail Bombing' in the *Guide to Netiquette*.

The cause of the trouble was a two-megabyte file with which someone had decided to electronically constipate Mr Newbie's Internet link. It took almost an hour to download onto his computer, during which time Mrs Newbie kept poking her head round the door and saying she hoped he wasn't turning into one of those Internet pornographers that she'd heard about on the news.

The e-mail was headed 'Compuserve Asshole!'. After a long while scrutinising his dog-eared copy of the popular reference book *Big Computers Guide for the Mentally Challenged* he managed to work out how to decode it by clicking on the big grey button marked 'Decode'. The file was, naturally enough, an enormous full-colour close-up of an unidentified baby. It was accompanied by the following short but to the point note, which had also been posted to news.newusers.questions.

```
From: KewlSurfer@aol.com
Re: LamerZ!


Jeez! U r such a lamer! Why dont u learn 2
use the net properly or better still just go
screw yourself u compuserve lamer. Newbies
like u really make me mad, u r so lame.
Don't u know it is a waste of band width
posting Me Too messages? This news group is
for kewl questions like what is FTP and how
do u use it? (if any 1 knows the answer 2
this pleez mail me at KewlSurfer@aol.com).
Not lame questions like yourz.

Go back 2 lamerville, u lame lamer.
```

L8r

KewlSurfer ;-)))

PS. IF 4nYbodY hAz wArEZ siTeZ pleeZ mAiL mE
kOz I M EL33t aNd tOTaLLy K-rAD d00d.

The message was signed with a 10-line ASCII graphic of Bart Simpson picking his nose. Mr Newbie wasn't a die-hard Simpson fan and assumed this to be a crudely drawn representation of Rodin's 'The Thinker'.

flaming

After another hasty consultation of the *Guide to Netiquette* he came to the conclusion that he'd probably been 'Flamed.' At first he wasn't too happy about this – then he realised that KewlSurfer@aol.com was patently one of these net.gods who'd been cruising the I-Way since the days when the MSN was just a tinkle in Bill Gates' wallet. Maybe he was a programmer – that would explain all those strange, coded references to 'wArEZ siTeZ'. Mr Newbie decided that, actually, he was privileged to be party to this digital denizen's words of wisdom. He posted back the following:

From: newbie@compuserve.com
Re: LamerZ!

Dear Mr Kewl Surfer

Thankyou for your kind advice. I am a

stranger to the ways of cyberspace but eager to learn - and flattered that someone of your standing could spare the time to assist a newcomer such as myself. The internet is indeed a fine model for society.

Kind Regards,

Mr Newbie

When he logged in that afternoon, his 'Free Sample Chapter' still hadn't arrived. But this had:

From: KewlSurfer@aol.com
      Re: LamerZ!

r u taking the piss or wot? Go get a FAQ.

KewlSurfer

PS. I hAv listZ oF w0rKinG sitEZ! wILl tRaD3 4 c0pY oF sIM ciTy! MAiL mE d00dz!

Mr Newbie had never been told to 'Go get a FAQ' before, although Kevin on the technical support phone line had said something awfully similar the night he called at 11.30pm to report that he'd accidentally deleted everything on his C:\ drive and wasn't sure which key to press to get it all back again.

As for the last line of the message, that didn't make sense even after he'd run it through his spell checker. Perhaps KewlSurfer was Norwegian. He tried again.

From: newbie@compuserve.com
Re: LamerZ!

Dear Mr Kewl Surfer

Unfortunately I do not know what a FAQ is - perhaps you would be kind enough to give me

one. As I said, unlike yourself I am merely
an enthusiastic amateur.

I see you are having problems with your Caps
Lock key. Have you thought of posting a
question to one of the Usenet newsgroups?
The people there seem very helpful.

Regards,

Mr Newbie

It was nearly 8pm, and Mr Newbie was already on his third
whisky of the evening when the last log-on of the day produced
this reply:

From: KewlSurfer@aol.com
Re: LamerZ!

SKREW U.

K-Surfer.

MR NEWBIE SENDS AN UNWISE E-MAIL

That was the final straw. Coincidentally, Demolition Man was
on the Sky Movie Channel. Mr Newbie had opened a bottle of
Scrumpy Jack Cider and was feeling pretty psyched up for
revenge. One day there will be a law against being drunk in
charge of a modem. It will begin as a civil suit for mental
harassment in California, but by the year 2010, when the
superhighway is no longer seen as a metaphor, legislation will
be implemented worldwide to keep the highway free of
inebriated surfers. Newbie sat down and tapped out his riposte.

From: newbie@compuserve.com
Re: LamerZ!

Dear Mr Kewl Surfer

Kindly stick your putrid, foul-mouthed head
up your own smug self-satisfied rectal

cavity, you scum-sucking piece of
Californian cyberpunk. I don't care how long
you've been on the Internet. According to
'Big Computers For the Logically Challenged'
there are over 40 million people on this
network and therefore you are no more
significant than a pus-filled pimple on the
acne-ridden face of society. Perhaps your
constant desire for exposure on the Internet
is caused by your having very small
genitalia?

Yours,

Mr Newbie

He went to bed feeling Empowered.

As soon as the alarm went off next morning Mr Newbie hurried
to the study, still in his pyjamas, and switched on the computer.
There was only one new message in news.newusers.questions.

From: KewlSurfer@aol.com
Re: LamerZ!

At 00.45 yesterday newbie@compuserve.com
wrote:

> Kindly stick your putrid, foul-mouthed
head up your own smug self->satisfied rectal
> cavity, you scum-sucking piece of
excrement. [...] >Perhaps your constant
desire
> for exposure on the Internet is caused by
your having very small >genitalia?

u r disgusting. i am forwarding this message
to postmaster@compuserve.com and hopefuly he
will have u cut off. i am a high school
student here in Kentucky and i have only
been on the net for a week. my mom and dad
got me a computer 4 my 13th birthday. dad

says people like u r perverts and should get
fried in the electric chair.

L8r

Kimberley (KewlSurfer@aol.com)

Mr Newbie was so shocked that he almost didn't notice Mrs
Newbie standing behind him and looking over his shoulder.

'So I was right!' she announced. 'You *are* one of those Internet
pornographers. I knew it!' And she unplugged his modem cable
from the phone socket, neatly snipped the plug off the end with
her nail scissors and stormed into the kitchen to ring his mother.

MR NEWBIE'S LIST OF USENET GROUPS (in order of popularity)

Newsgroup	No. of users per month
news.announce.newusers	1,000,000
rec.humor.funny	440,000
news.answers	430,000
news.newusers.questions	360,000
misc.jobs.offered	330,000
rec.humor	280,000
news.lists	250,000
alt.tv.simpsons	230,000
rec.arts.movies.reviews	230,000
rec.arts.startrek.current	230,000
rec.arts.startrek.info	210,000
alt.binaries.pictures.supermodels	200,000
rec.arts.startrek.misc	190,000
rec.arts.erotica	180,000
rec.radio.amateur.misc	180,000
rec.arts.movies	180,000
rec.video	180,000
misc.jobs.contract	180,000
misc.jobs	180,000
alt.music.alternative	170,000
alt.personals	170,000
rec.arts.startrek.tech	170,000

MR NEWBIE'S FAVOURITE WEB SITES

http://www.talon.net/newbie/ <usechoice@talon.net.>
The Newbies Corner home page is a long scrolling links list to
just about anything a newbie would need to know. Free
software – and loads of it – including Eudora and FTP and
browsers, one of which you presumably have already.

http://www.isisnet.com/mlindsay/nindex.html
The News of the wURLd site is a monthly magazine for new
newbies and those who never graduate from being newbies and
therefore require a monthly update.
mlindsay@ra.isisnet.com

http://www.netwelcome.com/index.html
A giant handshake welcomes the newbie to the Netwelcome
home page. There then follows a polite introduction to
netiquette and everything you need to know and get to be on
the Net (assuming you're not already).
dcrowder@bridge.net

http://www.Yinspire.com/
A non-techno techno page for newbies and technophobes.
The site lists and pictures women, seniors, families and small
business owners and their pets, one of which the newbie will
identify with.

Chapter

8

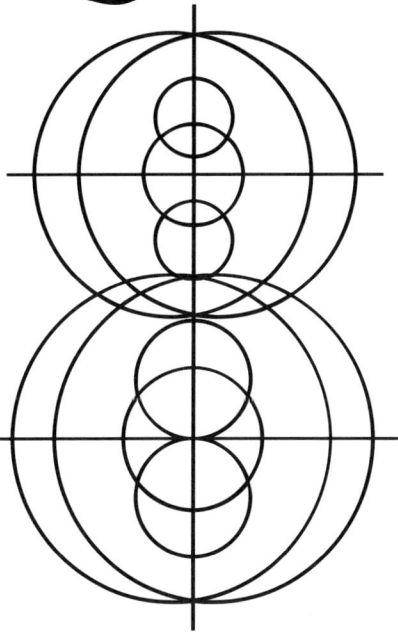

JUNIOR INTERNET

Snap-crackle-pop.com
Bert sneaks a peek at the Web
Bert's favourite Web sites
Engaged tone hell – the
one-phone household
Netiquette – Don't use big
SIGs
On the Internet things may not
be what they seem
Bert is nearly subjected to
virtual sex
Free software to block access
to porn
Music on the Web
Bert's favourite music sites
Music Mags on the Web

BERT'S FIRST EXPERIENCE OF BEING A 'HOME-USER'

The next day was the first of the half-term holiday. That morning at breakfast Mr Newbie had been meaning to warn Bert against going Net-surfing on his own. But the effects of the several gallons of coffee he had drunk the night before to keep alert while tinkering with his computer settings meant he had only fallen asleep at 5am. Three hours later he was definitely not feeling at his best. He certainly did not feel like talking to Bert, who was eating Rice Krispies and reading the box – 'www.snap-crackle-pop.com', it said on the label.

As a result, Mrs Newbie was entirely unaware that Bert had the electronic world at his fingertips. Mrs Newbie was in awe of computers. After reading a series of articles on the *Daily Express* Technology page, she had wanted the household to get on the Net for the sake of their son's education. There were also a few secret ideas of her own that she wanted to try.

While she continued with her part-time home-office job of market-research recruiter, Bert climbed the stairs and logged on.

The Rice Krispies packet had been unexpectedly informative about KidNet, one of the cereal's pick of the top ten snappiest, crackliest, popest Web sites for kids.

He typed in the URL, the unique address that identifies each Web site. The Netscape browser hummed for a moment and then told him that successful contact had been made with the host computer in British Columbia, Canada.

Little seemed to happen after that. Bert tapped his fingers on the desk. Had the computer crashed again? Or had the connection failed? At last some numbers appeared in the bottom left of the screen telling him that files were being downloaded. The process lasted a whole five minutes. Finally the screen was filled with a huge graphic saying 'KidNet'. There were brightly

coloured 'links' to other pages and Bert got down to the serious task of exploring the world of kids on the Net.

BERT'S FAVOURITE KIDS SITES

http://plaza.interport.net/kids_space/index.html contact
via:http://plaza.interport.net/kids_space/mail/forms/formM.html
Animated teddy bears, flowers and kids welcome you to Kidspace. Stories, galleries and real-time audio make this site very interactive.

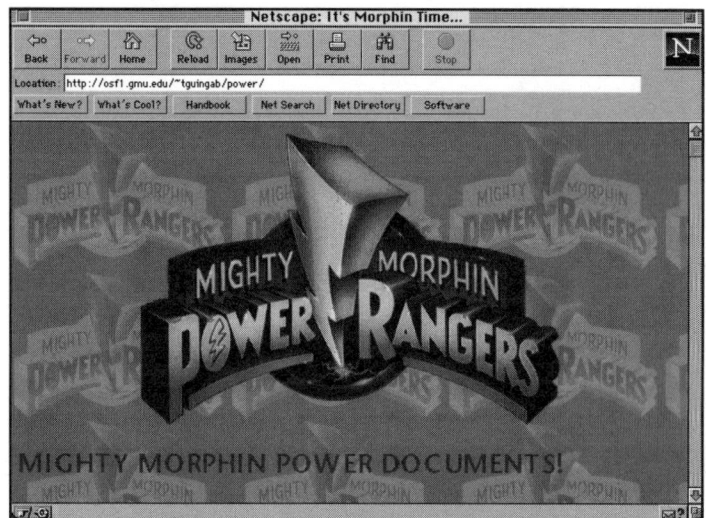

http://osf1.gmu.edu/~tguingab/power/
The unofficial Mighty Morphin Power Rangers Web site. FAQs and links to related sites as well as a complete episode guide to each series.
tguingab@osf1.gmu.edu

http://psych.hanover.edu/kidsweb/
Cool site for kids: post birthday messages, post your own art work and make e-mail penpals. Links to space and dinosaurs.
krantzj@hanover.edu

http://www.webcom.com/reeduk/thomas/
Thomas the Tank Engine – every kid's favourite story on the Internet.
cd16@dial.pipex.com

ENGAGED TONE HELL

Downstairs, Mrs Newbie was compiling the results of last night's in-depth market research discussion group. The man from P&O Cruises had been very pleased with the response. Eight couples had attended in the Newbie living-room, each answering questions about the food they would like to eat while on a 10-day Mediterranean cruise. Mrs Newbie managed to make a profit of £92.80 – £10 per couple and £12.80 on the food and drink, which she had bought in under budget.

Pleased with this triumph, Mrs Newbie waited impatiently for P&O to phone through with details of the next assignment. The call should have come an hour ago. If she had thought to check the phone, Mrs Newbie would have heard the unmistakable high-pitched screeching of a modem connecting to an Internet provider.

Upstairs, Bert had taken a complex route – following a dozen links – and found himself in a live kids chat session on the IRC. Internet Relay Chat is an acquired taste. There are hundreds of IRC channels, each an anarchic, real-time gossip-tank, where sentences typed in from all over the world fly up the screen.

NETIQUETTE
NET-CADET: DON'T USE
BIG .SIGs!

Bert was busy composing an e-mail to one of his friends in the States, comparing their prowess at various games and bemoaning

the uncoolness of their respective Dads. The e-mail was tagged with Bert's '.sig' – a short file that's used to personalise mail and news postings. Some people like to put an employer's disclaimer like 'The opinions expressed in this e-mail are not necessarily those of Microsoft Ltd' or a quote from some renowned intellectual or philosopher such as Mr Spock of Star Trek.

Bert's .sig went as follows:

This message is Copyright (c) BERT 'The Kewlest Kid On The Net' (TM) 1996 :-)

Quote: 'Uhuhhuhh. Huhuhuhu. Uhuh. Huh. Huhuhuhhuhuhuhhhhuh.'
    - Butthead, 'Beavis and Butthead,' MTV.

E-mail: Bert@powerranger.demon.co.uk
WWW:
http://www.compuserve.com/homepages/Bert/mypage.htm
Phone: Not when my Dad is in!!!! :-(
Snail mail: 10 Council Cottages,
            Basildon,
            England,
            Great Britain,
            UK,
            The World,
            The Solar System,
            The Universe,
            The Net,
            Cyberspace

DEATH TO ALL PARENTS!!!!!

Norbert stopped him just as he was about to click on 'Send Mail'.

'You do know you're not supposed to have a .sig more than four lines long?'

'Uhuh.' Bert shrugged nonchalantly and decided to change the e-mail by adding a few extra noughts to his claimed High Score on Lemmings.

Norbert tried to adopt a vaguely authoritative tone of voice and sternly addressed the back of Bert's head.

'Long .sigs are nothing more than a waste of bandwidth. How many e-mails do you post in a day?'

'139' responded Bert without looking up.

bytes
>>>FREE SCREENING FOR PARENTS

The researcher credited with starting the World Wide Web says he'll offer a free screening program to people who want to keep objectionable material from entering their computers from the Internet.

Tim Berners-Lee, director of the World Wide Web Consortium at the Massachusetts Institute of Technology, says he would rather see parents control what their children access instead of relying on broad censorship.

The Web was a universal information medium of great importance and potential and it should not be constrained by government fiat, he said.

http://www.w3.org/pub/WWW/

'Or more.'

'So, just think of all the unnecessary text you're sending. All you really need in a signature file is your name, and maybe the name of the person you work for. You don't even need to tell people where they can e-mail you because that's added to the top of the message automatically.'

Bert grunted. He wasn't convinced.

'Listen. Imagine if all the forty million people on the Internet had .sig files as long as yours. The Information Superhighway would just become one massive traffic jam.'

'Yeah? Great! Then Dad would use all those naughty words like when he drives me to school in the rush hour.'

Norbert gave up on kids.

His first words were "World Wide Web"

ON THE INTERNET NOTHING IS NECESSARILY WHAT IT SEEMS

After half an hour Bert grew bored of introducing himself to other kids from around the world and answering a host of similar questions about London. 'Don't foreigners realise there's a lot more to Britain than London?' he wondered as he looked at a clickable map of the UK and saved the address into his bookmark file so he could access it easily the next time one of the IRCers started asking him about the geography of England.

'Hello,' he typed to a newcomer called PeeWee from New York. 'I'm on my Dad's computer. Do you like Tank-girl?'

'Yeah' typed PeeWee. 'She's just like I want to be when I grow up.'

'You mean you're a girl?' typed back Bert in consternation.

'Yeah. I'm using my Dad's computer too. He's 58, and I'm 31.'

If Bert had been having this conversation within Kidlink's moderated forum, an alert adult systems operator might have intruded on the conversation and ended it straight away. But he was on an unregulated IRC channel and, although he did not know it, Bert was about to be offered a return air fare to San Francisco. But there was an interruption.

His mother appeared in the doorway. 'Are you playing Doom again?' she asked nervously, though anyone who has ever seen Doom would know that it does not include tourist maps of the United Kingdom.

'No Mum' replied Bert as he hurriedly switched to the *Times* home page.

Mrs Newbie saw the red lights on the modem flashing. She didn't know what a modem was, but she could see the box was connected to the phone line; instinctively she knew that those flashing red lights were the cause of her unrequited two-hour wait for instructions from P&O.

'Are you on the phone with that thing?' she snapped. He sighed as she switched off the power supply to the modem. Bert had lost the chance of worldwide media exposure – 'Kiddie-Porn E-mail Scandal'. It would have been bigger than 'Kiddie Internet Addiction'. Just as his mother was about to question him closely about the phone charges for the Internet, the phone

⬆ ⬇ ➡ ⊞

started ringing.

The man from P&O was sarcastic. 'Been having a nice gossip-session?' Mrs Newbie did not try to explain about the Internet. She took down the details and hurriedly dressed to go down to the shopping centre and recruit the evening quota.

As soon as she nipped out, Bert was back on the Net. This time he headed straight for the music on the Web.

MUSIC ON THE WEB

Knowing the difference between Coolio and Ol' Dirty Bastard is crucial to your street cred when you're twelve years old. It's the difference between being laughed at and being respected. Bert needs some cred, something to set him apart from the *Smash Hits* readers in his class. Now, what would really impress them? Knowing all the words to the latest Wu Tang Wu Tang Clan tune? Knowing what Bjork's favourite ice cream is? Or what DJ Rap's top ten tracks of the month are?

The Net puts all the world's music knowledge at your fingertips, as Bert points out to his Greek pen friend, Yannis:

'Yannis,
How's it going? Just thought you outta know that you don't have to listen to that crap bazouki music any more. You can chuck out you're one Bob Marley CD and access loads of Reggae on the Net.
When are you gonna persuade your Mum and Dad to get hooked up?
It would be cool cos then you'll know what I'm talking about when I say that Drum n Bass is the lick. The Net explains it all. Also, I wouldn't have to bother writing to you, I could E-mail you.
Anyway, I'm off to visit Echobelly (if you had the Net, you'd know who they are).
See ya (and I wouldn't wanna be ya),

Bert.'

Here's some of the links Bert got his grubby little hands on:

NET-CADET'S LIST OF FAVOURITE MUSIC SITES

Bert's favourite label site is Def Jam because it has loads of little quotes from the stars peppering the pages.

'From the label that brought you LL Cool J, Public Enemy, EPMD, Method Man, RedMan and all the other phat flavors, we're bringing that same flavor to the Net. We coulda came soft, but we carry a big stick... Givin' ya' full graphics on da Net like we're suppoze to... So come walk da' streets wit' us, we got ya' back!'

It's full of quotes, sound bites and graffiti-style art – big and bold – which works well on the Net. Artists vary from hardcore rappers Onyx to Ragga's self-acclaimed prophet Capleton. Here are the categories you get to choose from: Def Jam Biography, New Releases, Artist Info, Tour Info, Multimedia Discography, Newsletter and Mail.
Def Jam is at http://www.defjam.com/defjam/

By the way, if you don't understand some of the lingo on this site, then just do what Bert did: go to the Rap Dictionary (http://www.sci.kun.nl/thalia/rapdict/). Here you can find out what a 'double deuce juice' is, or you could get shot trying to order a drink.

Def Jam is part of Polygram, which is also on the Net. You can download song samples and video clips as well as information on new releases. You're bound to bump into Dwight, Polygram's cartoon mail-room boy (who's also in a band called Keyless Chucks, performing classics such as 'I Need You Like A Guitar Solo'). He adds a bit of colour to the site and looks good even on 4 megabytes of RAM. You can browse through an artist or genre list (Pop, Urban, Dwight, Alternative, Rock, Country, Classical, Soundtrack and Jazz).
Polygram is at http://www.polygram.com/polygram/

But Bert is a patriot at heart, so he often finds himself at Go!Discs, a UK label on the Net. Artists include Portishead, Paul Weller and Lisa Moorish.

Go!Discs are at http://www.godiscs.co.uk

Underground Music Archive
http://www.iuma.com/IUMA

Supersonic Guide to British Indie Music
http://www.freestyle.com/supersonic/

Internet Music Resource Guide
http://www.teleport.com/~celinec/mus_gnrl.htm

Yahoo Artists List
http://www.yahoo.com/Entertainment/Music/Artists

Black Pages Music Links Page
http://www.gatech.edu/bgsa/blackpages/music.html

The UK Top 40
http://www.glas.apc.org/~yook/ukchart.htm

The UK Singles
http://www.dotmusic.com/uksingle.html

Funky Site of the Day
http://www.realitycom.com/cybstars/index.html
Sometimes it's a music site, but whatever it is it's always funky.
This site is a helpful tool in gaining web cred – bookmark the
week's funky sites and relax in your coolness.

MTV
http://www.mtv.com/
Choose from: Out From Underground, Where's The Beat,
Music Feature, Sonic Stew, Reviews, Top 20, Buzz Clips, Heavy
Rotation, 120 Minutes, Gossip Guru, Bits & Bytes, 7 Days of
Music.

Bert's a bit of a Jungle fan and loves to chat to other Junglists
via The World Wide Jungle page
(http://durhamnet.com/jungle/).

Bert has catholic tastes. He webbed over to the Dub home page

(http://mw3.com/electro/dub-pg.htm), which has links to other
underground music sites.

Bert has a crush on Bjork, and all her Web sites are in his
bookmarks. He's waited 10 minutes to download a ten-second
sample… he must be in luuuurve!
Find Bjork at http://www.bjork.co.uk/bjork/

He doesn't like Blur; all the girls in his class fancy Damon,
which makes him feel jealous.
Blur are at http://www.musicbase.co.uk/blur/

Oasis are OK because they've got Denis Healey eyebrows and
they're lads. Bert thinks they're tough, even though he has no
idea what a 'Wonderwall' is.
Find them at http://www.cts.com/browse/ginger/

Apart from Bjork, Bert's other loves are Janet Jackson
(http://www.mit.edu:8001/people/agoyo1/janet.html),
and Junglist sex symbol DJ Rap
(http://www.demon.co.uk/djrap/).

Bert's parents managed to sneak in a few music bookmarks.
Dad's choice was BB King's site (http://bbking.mca.com/),
which wasn't too uncool for Bert. Mum's choice, on the other
hand, was grossly embarrassing. If Bert says 'Swedish pop
group from hell', Mum knows who he's talking about. Yes, it's
ABBA (http://phymat.bham.ac.uk/ABBA/). Bert was shocked to
find out that his Mum had also subscribed to the Abba
Newsgroup (news:alt.music.abba). What if one of his friends
were to look through his bookmarks and find ABBA? It was
worse than buying the wrong trainers (www.nike.com).

At Geffen/DGC Records the dark backgrounds reflect the
flavour of the music – artists include Nirvana, Slash's Snakepit,
Elastica, Hole, Jawbreaker, Urge Overkill and Veruca Salt.
When Bert wants to get a little morbid and wallow in his
pre-pubescent angst, this is the place he visits.
Find them at http://geffen.com/

To see which newsgroups suit you, access the whole list of
music newsgroups at:

http://www.edv.agrar.tu-muenchen.de/news/alt.music.html
From Beethoven to Black Sabbath, Lloyd Weber to Leonard
Cohen, Mariah Carey to Mods – they're all here.

LIST OF MUSIC MAGAZINES

As for music magazines, you need never buy another glossy,
over-priced, environmentally unfriendly paper thing again. The
Net has magazines galore:

I-Times – http://www.i-times.co.uk/it
Pop-i – http://www.webbiz.com/POPI/
4080 – (pure hip-hop)
http://www.hooked.net/buzznet/4080/index.html
The Beat –
http://www.owlnet.rice.edu/~don/press/beat.html
Addicted to Noise (all types) –
http://www.addict.com/ATN/
Gavin – http://www.iuma.com/gavin/
Grand Royal Magazine –
http://www.nando.net/GrandRoyal/Magazine/
Grooves –
http://pathfinder.com/@@jhR4KQE04wAAQEh9/
grooves/
Hip-Hop Connection – http://www.musicians-
net.co.uk/HHC/HHC.html
Keep It Real –
http://www.charm.net/~ces/keep_it_real/
RetroActive Baggage (Warwick University's leading
quality music publication) –
http://www.csv.warwick.ac.uk/~maurj/
Seconds – http://www.iuma.com/Seconds/
The Source –
gopher://gopher.enews.com:70/11/magazines/alpha
betic/su/source
Streetsound – http://www.streetsound.com.zone/
Tribe – http://www.io.org/~tribe/

Vibe – http://www.vibe.com/
X Magazine – http://michaeljones.uoregon.edu/
Progression – http://www.gold.net/users/ex14
Festival Focus (UK Music Festivals) –
http://194.72.60.96/www/festivals/index.htm
Oculus – http://www.oculus.com/oculus
London Calling – http://www.demon.co.uk/london-
calling/filmmus.htm

Chapter

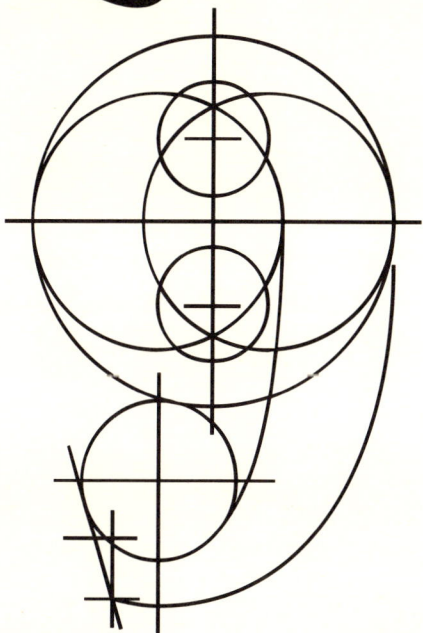

In search of a social life

World's shortest e-mail address

Net-vet's favourite Web sites

Norbert faces up to Internet addiction

GETTING TO KNOW NORBET

NORBERT THE NET-VET IN SEARCH OF A SOCIAL LIFE

Apart from his phone bills, Norbert's major item of expenditure is cannabis. He likes to get stoned and surf the Web or play the role of Muffin the Mule in a multi-user dimension.

Once a month he goes to a pub in Lamb's Conduit Street to drink real ale with others of his kind. They are all subscribers to Demon, one of the rawest, most techie Internet link-ups available in the UK. Demon is a strange phenomenon: the most popular dial-up service in the UK, yet its help-desk phone lines are always busy and its Internet connections are rarely 100%. It was an early UK indicator that there was money to be made out of the Internet – at least for the stockbrokers, who took millions in fees when they placed Demon's shares, valuing it at £28 million.

None of this is on the minds of the programming-hardened veterans as they drink their way through a Demon 'meet'. They look at the surroundings with a surprised air, as though they don't get out very often. And none of them could be described as fashion victims.

WHO HAS THE WORLD'S SHORTEST E-MAIL ADDRESS?

When a few Net-vets get together the chat is of such mind-numbing tinyness as to be almost inconceivable. Like this recent

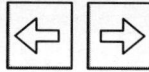

exchange from a discussion group devoted to Net people:

```
Newsgroups: soc.net-people
Subject: Re: Who has the shortest e-mail
address?
Date: 29 Aug 1994 19:58:41 GMT
Organization: Bolt Beranek and Newman, Inc.
Lines: 21
Message-ID:
<LEVIN.94Aug29155841@cassandra.bbn.com>
References: <33q55h$210a@whale.st.usm.edu>
<1994Aug29.183032.12009@sq.sq.com>
NNTP-Posting-Host: cassandra.bbn.com
In-reply-to: msb@sq.sq.com's message of Mon,
29 Aug 94 18:30:32 GMT

> Who has the shortest, fully-qualified e-
mail address ...

Of people who post frequently in groups I
read, the shortest addresses
seem to belong to Dik T. Winter
(dik@cwi.nl) and me. I have encountered at
least one shorter one, but I don't remember
who it was.

<snip>

Well, I know someone whose e-mail address is

   <user>@x.org

where <user> is his five letter last name
(which I am keeping out for
the usual reasons).

If someone there were known by a two- or
three-letter user-id that
person would probably hold the record.

<snip>
```

Organization: Customer Account on MCSNet, Chicago, Illinois 60657-3200

Paul Vader, who is both pv@mcs.com and pv@wwa.com, would be tied with Mark and Dik.

<snip>

dattier@MCS.COM (David W. Tamkin) writes:

I know someone who is xx@rtp.uk. 'xx' takes the place of his
initials, of course.

Norbert spends a great deal of time thinking about his 'sig ' file – the section at the end of the messages where Net-heads usually include a quote that sums up their 'philosophy' along with their many addresses and phone numbers.

For example:

Paul W. Cashman, vanyel@crl.com Rush Dream Theater Queensryche
Metallica Hawkwind Enya Ministry Mutha's Day Out Sisters of Mercy Dead Can Dance Blue Oyster Cult
'You see me locked in my closet / That's where I'll make my stand...'

NET-VET FAVOURITE SITES

http://www.corcom.com/reloj/Nerdnosh.html
Sit around a virtual campfire and check out some of the nerdiest people you're ever likely to meet.
klatsch@nerdnosh.org

http://www.cyberzine.com/webcomics/nerd/index.html
A nerd-a-bird in Brazil spends all his time on a computer.
A comic strip nerd and his friends; updated regularly.

gompy@lsi.usp.br

http://www.students.uiuc.edu/~w-tyczk/

The page opens with an impressive photograph entitled 'Molecule of the month'. Lots of pure science links as well as financial and church links.
w-tyczk@students.uiuc.edu

NORBERT FACES UP TO INTERNET
Addiction

After a continuous nine hours sitting in front of his computer terminal, Norbert wondered if what he really needed was an Internet addiction clinic. One had opened in Maryland that week; perhaps it would become a celeb detox hangout like Michael Douglas' sex addiction clinic – he might even meet Stephen Fry or Billy Idol. Maybe soon we'll be able to buy 'Quit Browsing In 30 Days' on a CD-ROM…

Net-Veterans have not really taken to the wave of consumer CD-ROMs, but they have *great* fun tweaking the computer hard drive and rewriting .exe files to make the CD-ROMs run better.

As Norbert paused to consider writing a draft treatment for his CD-ROM 'Computer Addiction Cure' the lights went out and the radio stopped. The smooth hum of the negative-ion generator (which he used to minimise the harmful electric cloud that permanently surrounded him) ended in a strangulated squeak. Only the computer kept whirring, and the screen bathed his face in a surreal light. 'Thank heavens for the uninterruptable power supply' thought Norbert, who had invested in the special plug which ensures that in the event of a power failure there is enough in reserve to keep working for another 20 minutes and save all the currently open files to avoid losing any data.

He switched over to his NU-soft personal secretary, the database he used for household administration. He had it programmed to send out cheques precisely 30 days after the bill was received. Perhaps something had got out of sequence. But no, there it

was. The software had indeed printed out a cheque for the electricity board on the 30th day after the bill had arrived. But now he thought about it the letter hadn't been posted for a few days because he kept forgetting to buy stamps. The cheque must have arrived after the order went out for him to be disconnected. Norbert was furious. Another example of the mechanical bureaucracy that couldn't even get its mechanics together.

He decided to use the remaining few minutes of his power supply to send a furious letter. The power died the moment the internal fax modem finished transmitting. Now Norbert was confronted with a major dilemma – what to do instead? He couldn't watch TV; not that that was any loss – he never watched TV anyway. He tried reading a book, but it made him want to log on and tell his friends on alt.books what he thought about it. By 9am the next morning Norbert was in the canteen of the local technical college ready to bribe anyone who would let him telnet from their machine into his own e-mail account.

A few days later, in the North Devon office of the electricity company, the head of accounts was scratching his head over the letter Norbert had sent.

'Strangest thing,' he murmured as his assistant placed the morning coffee on his desk. 'The guy seems to be able to spell all right but the letter is just unintelligible. Look at all this gobbledegook… IMHO, WBFTHHHG. And what are all these dots and brackets and colons doing all over the place?' As his assistant's boyfriend had an e-mail account, she was able to explain that the weird symbols were 'smilies', the emoticons that Net-heads use to decorate their pages. IMHO meant 'in my humble opinion'. It seemed that, under time pressure, Norbert had used Internet language for his Outernet correspondence. A natural mistake to make if you spend more than 80 hours a week on-line.

'Oh, well, he seems to be right. He paid up last week', said the accounts boss. 'Turn the power back on.'

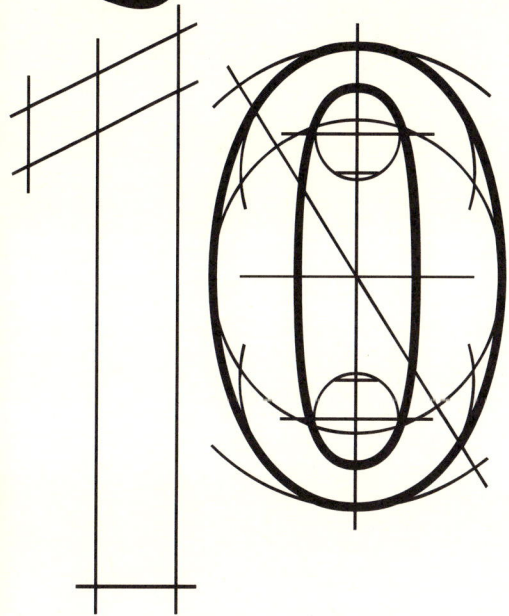

Chapter #10

NET PROFITS

- 10 ways to tell a Net-profiteer
- Vanessa Fox – Get rich quick
- Cigarettes on the Net
- Sexy GIFs
- Dirty talk
- $200 billion sales forecast
- Samaritans online
- Profiteers' favourite Web sites
- Make money fast
- City report is the Profiteers' bible
- Vanessa gets herself a name
- Vogue-net?

Vanessa is often to be found perched on a high stool in Harvey Nichols' chic fifth-floor bar, a cigarette dangling from her lips, composing e-mail to her (dwindling number of) online admirers. She sees the Net as the ideal way to recapture her halcyon days as a glamorous and much-fancied party-going good-time girl. Even with the size of her phone bill it's a lot cheaper than a face lift.

She is constantly fascinated by big money's arrival on the Net, and she specialises in taking no moral stand. Cigarettes, for example, are not banned in her house.

Vanessa's Internet low point came when she accidentally deleted the file BLONDE.GIF, a digitised photograph of herself as she was 15 years earlier, which she'd been cross-posting to various Usenet groups (soc.personals, alt.singles, alt.singles.uk, alt.binaries.pictures.erotica). Now she has to make do with a photo of her as she is now, which doesn't generate the same response. One of her former admirers cruelly re-posted it to alt.binaries.pictures.erotica.tasteless.

Laid out beside her PC are several mouse mats on which she stands bottles of cheap white wine. Discovering that one could order cases of wine from Sainsburys and get them delivered without even leaving your desk was the thing that first convinced her that the Net was going to be Something Big. She can easily get through two or three bottles in the course of a surfing session – she only logs off when her typing becomes so bad that no-one can understand her.

She posts sub-Mills-and-Boon erotic stories to alt.sex.stories under the pseudonym 'Fantasia'. These all revolve around the experiences of a glamorous, blonde, twenty-something PR woman who gets invited to lots of really good parties and meets really hunky guys who immediately want to go to bed with her. They have titles like 'Vanessa's Riding Lesson' and 'Vanessa's Wet Weekend'. She's only just been informed that these newsgroups are probably monitored by state officials.

She has absolutely no respect for the culture or customs of the Net, which is not surprising because she has no respect for anyone in Real Life either.

Vanessa is delighted at the lack of women on the Net since this means she's more likely to be chatted up by sad men on the IRC. She spends a lot of time having stilted, one-sided conversations with foreign people over the Internet phone (which often go something like this: 'I'm Vanessa and I'm a blonde. Where are you?' or 'Sorry <CRACKLE>, can you <HISS> repeat that please?').

Vanessa has embarked upon several doomed Internet ventures, including the country's first cyber wine bar, which had to close down due to lack of clientele – most of the nerds who visited it failed to meet her strict dress code and only bought soft drinks. She also attempted to sell a range of beauty and skincare products over the Net, which never took off either despite the large photograph and personal recommendation from herself on the Website.

Vanessa is seriously emotionally unstable and can't understand why she seems unable to hold down a relationship. She's given up going out with guys in Real Life since discovering video conferencing. She's hoping that the quality of the pictures doesn't get much better. In grainy black-and-white slow motion she still looks a bit of a stunner.

Bytes

A small but growing number of sites on the Internet's World Wide Web allow consumers to order cigarettes and other tobacco products. Major tobacco companies have shied away from setting up marketing Web sites, and Philip Morris, which last year launched a campaign to limit youth's access to cigarettes, says it actively opposes the practice.

Although the new Web sites tend to be shoestring operations, tobacco critics view them as a significant health threat. The Centre for Media Education, a non-profit child-oriented consumer group that has

She hangs out on the IRC simultaneously, frequenting the channels #blondes, #redheads, #brunettes, #twentysomething and #sexchat. She's involved in several online affairs at the same time – she just CC:s her explicit messages to all of them and waits for the response. She's currently corresponding with most of the Computer Science department at Washington University.

She recently discovered that the Samaritans are online. This was bad news for the Samaritans. They have now blacklisted her e-mail

address and every time she sends them another of her lengthy, tortuous late-night messages full of drunken angst, it just bounces straight back with an <Error: message not delivered> header. But it gave Vanessa the idea that she could set herself up as an online agony columnist, and she persuaded the editor of a webzine on a California university site to give her a weekly page called 'Dear Vanessa' to answer people's problems.

Following the tragic death of one of her regular readers, she received an e-mail saying that her column would no longer be required.

VANESSA'S FAVOURITE WEB SITES

http://www.moneyworld.co.uk/
The UK personal finance Web site. A complete on-line financial service for the UK. How to benefit from tax loopholes and the best places to put your money. Contact: http://www.moneyworld.co.uk/feedback.htm

http://www.ezlink.com/~peted/tmc.html

>>>CIGARETTES ARE BEING MARKETED THROUGH WEB SITES

complained to the Food and Drug Administration about the Web sites, terms them 'a completely unregulated media environment'. The FDA's proposed rule on tobacco marketing bans all cigarette-vending machines and mail-order sales but doesn't specifically address the issue of Internet sales. Moreover, the Federal Trade Commission's requirement that cigarette ads carry the Surgeon General's warning applies only to manufacturers; the Web sites – run mainly by tobacco retailers – for the most part aren't covered and rarely run such warnings.

http://www.elink.net/smoke/

GET RICH QUICK

IT'S SUPER HIGHWAY ROBBERY!

Publicity) at the address www.fox-up.com. She publicises this by inundating Usenet with lots of messages saying '***New Site With Hot XXX GIFs! ***'.

When she comes across a copy of 'The Internet in 1996 – an investment perspective', this becomes her bible as she attends meeting after meeting to promote her online business ideas.

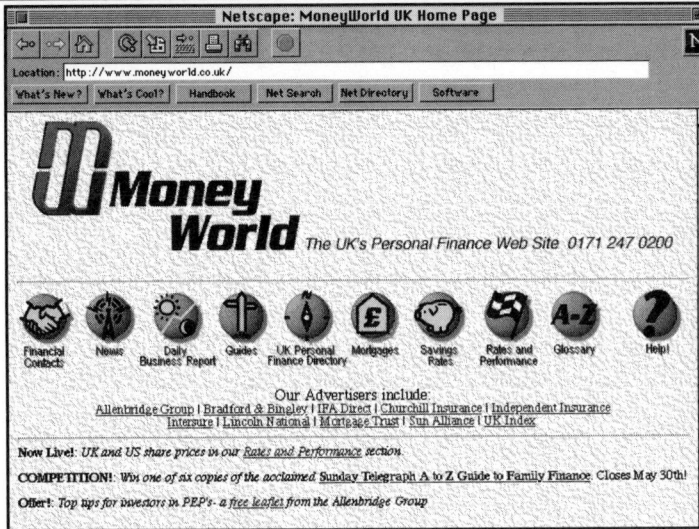

A Get Rich Quick here's how. Set up a Web site called 'Money course' and sell it over the Internet.

http://www.worldprofit.com/

Dr Jeffrey Lant's World Profit Malls, a database of hundreds of pages with free offers on how to maximise profit in every possible way.
incor@oanet.com.

MAKE MONEY FAST!!!

Vanessa's faith in online commerce was only slightly dented when she ordered something over the Net and had her credit card number stolen and used to call a lot of dirty phone lines in Brazil.

She's very excited at the prospect of virtual cash because she has very little real cash and is now exceedingly indebted on all her credit cards. She still manages to give the appearance of having money to burn, thanks to a combination of blagging, scamming, spamming and literally screwing cushy deals out of people.

She's just set up a Web site for her PR business (Fox United

Bytes >>> Intervid Report

EXECUTIVE SUMMARY

• The Internet is a global collection of connected computer networks. We forecast that there will be approximately 61.8 million users worldwide by year-end 1996, with commercial subscriptions growing at more than 100% per year.

• The UK market will grow from £35 million in 1995 to more than £900 million by the turn of the century. Current growth rates are more than 200% per annum.

• The WWW is doubling in size every three months. We forecast approaching 100,000 Web sites by the end of 1995, 75% of which will be based in North America.

• The most popular content of the Internet is still sex, and the biggest user group is the 25- to 34-year-old middle-class male. The next most popular subjects include research, travel and regional content.

• Business to business content is growing rapidly. Everything from multi-million pound computers to miles of oil pipeline to small magazine subscriptions are now being bought, sold and bartered via the Net.

• The Internet will be used for collecting and searching for data, video, voice communications and electronic mail, music, entertainment, watching live sport and movies, interactive television, retailing, advertising, market research, corporate and political PR, international cultural events, dealing on international stockmarkets and much more.

• Peripheral industries, like cybercafes and Web design and production, are likely to exceed £65 million in UK sales in 1996.

• The first wave of successful (i.e. profitable) Internet-related business will come from the following sectors: Internet access service provision, Internet software applications provision and Internet hardware applications provision (servers, modems etc.). The second wave will be dominated by content provision.

• There will be increased price competition in the Internet Service Provider (ISP) market as new entrants aim for significant market share. Most ISPs will not become profitable until 1997/98, when the overall market will be large enough to support a number of major players on fairly slim margins.

• There will be increased investment in ISPs over the next three or four years as they compete for a market of five million likely subscribers within the next seven years. ISPs are given breathing space by investors to drive market share upwards; thus, few ISPs are actually profitable at present.

• The largest ISPs will survive because of the economies of scale they can achieve in network operation, telecoms purchasing power, software discounting, etc. Smaller companies will either be taken over or will subsidise access services in order to secure value-added service provision, such as advertising, electronic publishing or Web page maintenance.

• The US stockmarkets are currently valuing ISPs at an average of 10-12 times current annual revenue. This values each subscriber at £1,500.

• The UK currently generates approximately 10% of all Internet turnover, which is approximately 33% of all non-USA revenues. By the end of the 1990s the United Kingdom's market share will have fallen to between five and six per cent.

• A move to audio and video in 1996 will put fresh strains on Internet bandwidth.

• Cable companies may be the main beneficiaries of the Internet because they have the bandwidth to deliver it at high speed.

• The alliance between News International, MCI and BT is one of several groupings that are planning a torrent of highly branded, well-structured Internet programming. This will be promoted by cross-marketing in News International media properties.

• Amateurs who stumble across the right formula for displaying content are already receiving 100,000 hits a day.

• The UK provider market is split into three groups – Corporate service providers offering leased line connections (UK market leader: Pipex), dial-up TCP/IP services (European market leader: Demon) and full-service online bulletin board services (BBS) offering add-on Internet access (European market leader: CompuServe).

• BT and Microsoft will eventually share at least 25% of the UK Internet market. Established providers will still have a good share as long as they provide a good standard of connectivity. This will partly be due to customer inertia (e.g. those with standing order accounts or who refuse to change e-mail address).

• The alliance between Microsoft, Pipex and U-Net is likely to gain significant market share in Europe.

• By 2002 we expect more than 200 million people worldwide to be connected to at least some parts of the Internet. We forecast 150 million global subscriptions to online services by 2002. Subscribers will use one of the following methods of connection:

direct access through an Internet access service provider, access through a full-service bulletin board service such as CompuServe or the Microsoft Network, connection through cable or satellite television links, and/or connection through a wireless telecoms provider on a mobile computing device.

• At present we estimate that less than 250,000 PC owners in the UK subscribe to a BBS service or have an account with an Internet service provider. This represents a market penetration of less than 5% today, or less than 2% of our market forecast for 1998 of 12.6 million PC owners.

• Hits are no longer seen as the authoritative yardstick of site popularity. 'Unique host access' is a better way of tracking audience statistics. Better still, all visitors to a Web page should be required to register. Then their response can be used to tailor individualised pages.

• EDI, the common standard for electronic data interchange within industry sectors, is being adapted for the Internet.

• The Internet is already providing duplex voice communication and will soon be capable of offering international calls at local prices (from a computer direct to a phone, rather than to another computer).

• Retail sales via the Internet are still very low but will be capable of commonly accepted security standards by mid-1996.

• The value of an Internet 'name' will increase.

VANESSA GETS HERSELF A NAME

There seemed to be a hierarchy based on your name, Vanessa concluded. For some reason people with e-mail addresses ending in 'aol.com' were treated like dirt by the rest of the Cyberspace community. Yet a completely tedious posting from someone called 'nick@itv.com' attracted several comments along the lines of 'wow, cool address' from the cybermorons that seemed to hang out in uk.singles.

After weeks of research, Vanessa paid out hundreds of pounds to register the names fox-up.com, santaclaus.com xmas.com. and reindeer.com. She intended to create a beautiful Christmas shopping mall on the net, and she had decided that Christmas 1996 would be Internet Christmas.

The arrival of the current month's *Vogue* magazine was always an important moment for Vanessa, offering the combination of a confirmation and a critique of her very existence. Would the fashion pages endorse or reject her choice of colours for autumn? Would the beauty column encourage her to think about a facelift or a hormone replacement? She always made sure she gave the magazine some quality time. After switching on the answering machine and saying goodnight to her online lovers, she studied the front cover. There in large letters were the words 'Harvey Nicks dot net'. This was news indeed! She turned to page 96.

'Will the Ladies Who Lunch And Don't Do Much Else end up slobbing around in dirty tracksuits, glued to their PCs to buy stuff online?' was the less-than-arresting opening sentence. 'Will customers at the Savoy ever be looking at the wine list via their Netscape hotlist?' She read on.

Harvey Nicks was apparently planning to put its entire catalogue online, but in an even more profound development they had decided to convert the famous fifth floor into the first haute-cuisine cybercafe.

Chapter

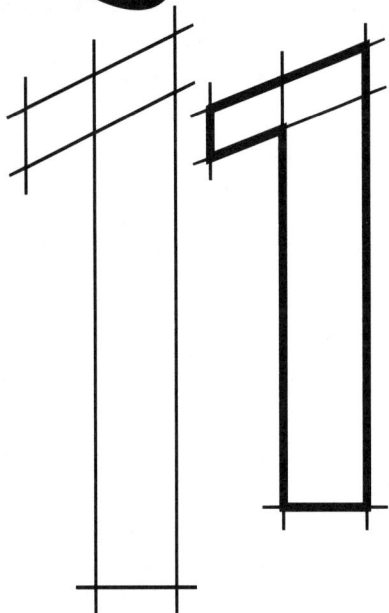

GEEK CHIC

The biggest Geek household in Santa Cruz

Groundhog Day Internet Divorce

Things that annoy Geeks

Netiquette… Don't flame Newbies

Favourite Geek sites

The Winnebiko – the world's biggest Geek project

Howard Vs Vanessa

HOWARD THE GEEK

Geeks are the fundamentalists, the purists of the Internet. They say they are defending the Net, which is being transformed by its new popularity.

They really believe the Internet is THEIRS. They invented it, they have been running it for the past decade, and now all these damned newbies are on the Net. To that extent they are prejudiced and are less qualified for the title 'Guardian of the Soul of the Internet' than the Net-veterans.

Net-heads to access their photos, their thoughts on everything and a constantly updated list of rave parties in the Santa Cruz area. Howard's room contains a bed and a selection of elderly computers in varying states of disrepair, which he takes apart from time to time with no discernible effect.

He is an anglophile, and spends hours on his hobby – constructing a computerised map of Britain featuring its pubs and archaeological sites. He now has 577 entries on his map. He is working on his next addition – to be called 'Kebab Corner' – a listing of all the greasy-spoon cafes in the country.

In this he is assisted by his fellow Geek – Sven from Stockholm. Sven has his own side-project, named 'Sven's Incredibly Cool Web Page', which leads any interested Net-heads to all sorts of obscure parts of the Net.

Sven has a £2500 high-end Pentium on which he only ever runs his Spectrum emulator program. He persists in trying to surf the Web using an old Amstrad and a 300-baud modem held together with rubber bands – and is inordinately proud of this achievement.

After spending half an hour waiting for his home page to load, he comes to the conclusion that everything on the Web takes far too long to download and is therefore All Crap. Sven's worst nightmare is that he loses his girlfriend to an online love affair.

Bright as a button despite his relatively advanced age of 37, Howard lives in Santa Cruz in a big house shared with other militant geeks. They have their own page on the Net – called 'The Biggest Geek household in Santa Cruz'. It allows other

THE MANY THINGS THAT BUG HOWARD THE GEEK

Howard enjoys hooking into the NASA space flight transmissions to keep up to date with what the astronauts are doing. Married and relatively sane, his main *bête noire* is the activities of the amateur Net-heads. He hates it when someone begins a message to a discussion group with the words 'This is a test'. And he hates the way they all ask the same questions – like 'Who owns the Internet?' September is the cruellest month for Howard because that is when a fresh intake of students are given their computer accounts and are able to flood the Net.

The other bad time is whenever one of the really big commercial parts of the Net (like CompuServe or America On-line) finally gives its subscribers full access to the Internet.

Something else that gets him really mad is when the Net is used for commercial purposes. When an Atlantic Records executive tried to advertise the new Nirvana CD on the Net, Howard and his friends reacted by 'mail-bombing' the offending Net-head – i.e. sending him megabyte-sized messages that tied up his computer for hours as well as causing severe problems to the offender's Internet provider company.

Bytes >>> GROUNDHOG DAY INTERNET DIVORCE

A New Jersey man who says he caught his wife having an affair on the Internet has filed for divorce. The wife and her alleged lover met on the Internet and were supposed to consummate their alleged illicit relationship on Groundhog Day in the US.

John Goydan of Bridgewater claims his wife, Diane, has been exchanging love letters for months with a married North Carolina man whose e-mail name is 'Weasel'.

Goydan's attorney, Richard Hurley, says Goydan came home from work early last October and caught his wife sending an X-rated message on the couple's home computer.

The computer-savvy Goydan recovered three months' worth of amorous messages and love poems and saved them on a disk.

Goydan says he did not let his wife know he was on to her. But when she arranged a secret rendezvous with Weasel at a bed and breakfast in New Hampshire on 2 February, Goydan decided he'd had enough.

http://ivory.lm.com/~donnpat/grhogday.html

NETIQUETTE...
DON'T FLAME NEWBIES

'It's that time of year again. Open season on newbies. I mean, you've got to flame them, haven't you; it's like natural selection, yeah? Otherwise the Net would be completely overrun with lamers who've just got their first Net-in-the-Box kit and think they know it all.'

Norbert thought this was rather unfair.

'Don't you think that's a bit harsh? You were a newbie once, remember?'

Howard spluttered black coffee onto his monitor screen and nibbled a Ginseng tablet.

'I was never a newbie. I *invented* the term "newbie". And they deserve all they get, the pathetic, whinging little... I mean, God, like everybody knows how to manually configure a TCP/IP stack, but these people still post stupid newbie questions. Hasn't anyone told them there's such a thing as netiquette?'

Norbert remained tactfully silent. Howard furrowed his brow behind thick-rimmed glasses and reached randomly for one of the cold, congealed slices of pizza that were gradually fusing with their containers. He took a bite out of a polystyrene carton but was too engrossed to notice.

'See this one here? Even his e-mail address is lame. Newbie@compuserve.com.

Someone should shoot the poor creatures at birth, if you ask me. Cull them. Like baby seals.'

'Now that's just being unfair. Newbies have a lot to bring to the Net. Diversity. New ideas. Instead of everyone in Cyberspace just being some sort of die-hard UNIX geek.'

'But you don't understand!' glowered Howard. 'Newbies are just so stupid! They do such... such *stupid* newbie things!'

He thumped the tabletop to emphasise his point. The computer slithered six inches to the right, the cable came out of its socket and Howard lost all the files he'd forgotten to save that evening.

FAVOURITE GEEK SITES

http://northshore.shore.net/~dreaming/
Derek's oddly unsettling zone. A personal home page including portrait of a geek as young man and a very geeky, short but sweet, real audio clip.
Lichter_Derek_D/svoa0001@ssb.com

http://www.ibmpcug.co.uk/~skcollob/puns.htm
Geek n Roll, the ultimate listing of famous music tracks that have been corrupted into geeky puns.
dabarham@skcollob.win-uk.net

http://www.next.com.au/spyfood/geekgirl/004maid/index.html
Myths and Mermaids, a geek girl site from Australia. A regularly updated e-zine, by geek-girls for geek girls.

http://www.resort.com/
The home page for a Geek house in Santa Cruz, Ca. Alien invaders have infiltrated human beings and drink gin by day, mutilate sheep by night.
resort@resort.com

See also
http://ruby.omg.org/mrktpl.htm
http://linex.com/~fenix/avian/ww.html
http://ucsub.colorado.edu/~armbrust/top10.html

PROJECT WINNEBIKO

Perhaps the strangest Geek project of all on the Internet is the Winnebiko and its successor, the Microship – a combined bicycle with computer.

Steven K. Roberts has now travelled nearly 20,000 miles on various trips around America on his solar-powered bicycle. Roberts pedals. The solar energy is reserved for his computer.

It started as a powerbook mounted on the handle bars and grew into a multi-million dollar research project with worldwide media coverage.

Here is an excerpt from Roberts' own Web page.

'Is there a central dream? Or am I just a gadget freak, propellerhead, and yuppie hobo all rolled into one, too set in my wandering ways to consider settling down?'

The Winnebiko project represents nearly $1.2 million worth of bicycle, including the value of professional time, and took 3.5 years to complete. About 150 corporate equipment sponsors, along with a couple of dozen occasional assistants, machinists, technicians and consultants, are involved.

It looks like an aircraft cockpit. Bristling with switches and LEDs, the Winnebiko II flickered into life in the summer of 1986. The primary design objective – being able to type while riding – had evolved into a mad tangle of processors and other sub-systems. The bike has a speech synthesizer that can be triggered by security sensors or remote radio command, a packet data communication system for e-mail via ham radio, solar panels generating 20 watts, an offline HP laptop, and more.

HOWARD VS VANESSA

While downloading the latest files from the comp.modems Usenet group, Howard came across a picture file – 'blonde.gif' – which was an oddity in a highly technical discussion group. It had been placed there by Vanessa, who hoped it would attract a Net-vet to contact her. She needed someone to fix her IRC software, which had been playing up recently. Instead she got Howard.

Howard's fury at Vanessa had to be instantly satisfied. He could only think of one thing – revenge. But a subtle revenge. He turned to the newsgroup alt.revenge for inspiration. This collection of sad but essentially harmless individuals liked to discuss the most intricate and complex of revenges to compensate for the indignities they suffered during their daily lives. There were the usual discussions of firecrackers in toilet bowls or newspapers wrapped around dog turds and set light to on front porches so the victim would try to stamp out the fire.

Vanessa's biggest client was the multinational engineering company Universal Shafting. She had made the point repeatedly in her postings and even included it in her sig for a while. Howard flicked his computer over to the Internic – the authority which handled all naming registration in the United States – and began typing rapidly. The next day he had an auto-mail back from the Internic confirming that universal-shafting.com, universal_shafting.com and universalshafting.com were registered names. This meant nobody else could use those names on the Internet, and since Universal Shafting had spent millions protecting its name, it was likely to feel pretty annoyed. With any luck, Vanessa would get rapped.

Vanessa might never even discover he had done this, thought Howard. But he knew. And that made him feel good. He would have felt even better if he had known that Vanessa was due to present her Internet proposal to the main board and that they would quickly have agreed to a £150,000 budget for the Universal Shafting home page. A few hours later still and Vanessa would be ashen-faced – her dreams of Net millions cruelly dashed once again.

Howard returned to his fantasy of being a Net-cop – easing his packet-sniffer out onto the infohiway and surfing the Web to keep filth at bay. The Newbies all called it the information superhighway – what a mouthful. He felt at ease '@ home', channel-surfing for trouble as the data packets streamed past him. He could see the unencrypted details of a thousand dirty secrets – enough information to start a thriving blackmail business. The Net was no longer a safe place for innocents.

Chapter

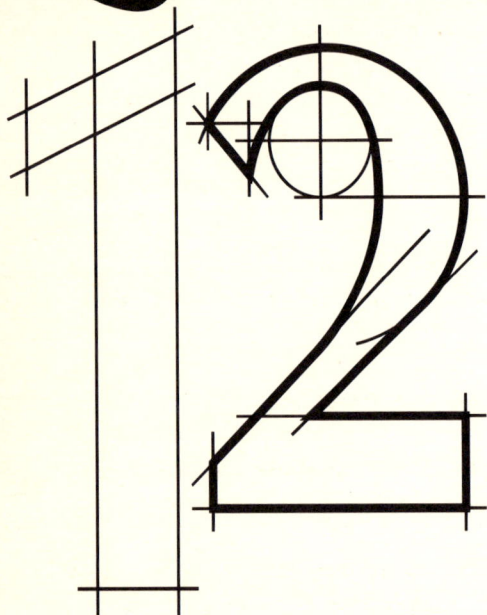

12

Netiquette: No spamming

Sisters unite for freedom

Cyber-harassment

Emoticons

Recycling

Feminist links

CHANGING THE WORLD

NETIQUETTE:
NO SPAMMING

Hettie the Net-activist had already fired off an urgent newsflash to the following list of top international journalists...

par@bbcnc.org.uk
wireduk@cityscape.co.uk
clive@vixen.demon.co.uk
mail@netguide.cmp.com>
netmag@futurenet.co.uk>
LisaH@computing.emap.co.uk>
paragon@itoday.demon.co.uk
libram@bonaly.hw.ac.uk
dickp@bix.com
edit@news.newsci.ipc.co.uk
thescopy@timesup2.demon.co.uk
obsscience@guardian.co.uk
jim_mcc@cix.compulink.co.uk
John@jdiamond.demon.co.uk
Tim.Jackson@pobox.com
innovations@telegraph.co.uk
innovation@delphi.com
100344.1032@compuserve.com
askbill@microsoft.com
steve@mcgook.demon.co.uk
nick@intervid.co.uk
online@guardian.co.uk

Now she was busy preparing her latest missive on behalf of one of the environmental pressure groups:

From: europa@whalesong.demon.co.uk
To: all@demon.co.uk
Newsgroups: alt.*, soc.*, rec.*, comp.*, uk.*
Re: GLOBAL DISASTER ABOUT TO HAPPEN

IMPORTANT: PLEASE READ IF YOU ARE CONCERNED ABOUT YOUR WORLD!

New research has concluded that in less than twelve years we could witness the extinction of the Common Sludge Worm. The Sludge Worm is native to many Eastern European countries and with your help we can help to protect this beautiful creature. NutNet, one of the Internet's ecological organisations, are in desperate need of donations and volunteers from all corners of Cyberspace...

[snip]

Norbert tapped her on the shoulder as she was about to post it.

'Er, who are you sending that to, Hettie?'

'I yam sending zis to efferybody who ees compassionate about ze environment.'

Hettie explained that she was also cross-posting it to a number of Usenet groups – 6000 approximately. Norbert was aghast.

'You can't do that! Spamming is one of the worst possible crimes you can commit against the Net community.'

Norbert was not exaggerating. The second-worst crime is to publish a Web site that applies the <BLINK> command to the entire page and begins with the phrase 'This page is only designed to work with Netscape 2.0 Beta Version 4 Build 15' (see the meeting between Norbert and the Netropolitan).

'I don't understand. I am ein Vegetarian. Vot ees zis "Spamming"?'

Norbert went on to describe the frankly obscene practice of posting the same article to hundreds of unsuspecting recipients and irrelevant newsgroups. It was the ideal way to guarantee yourself a flame-grilling from outraged Net-heads. At worst, everyone who read or received the message would forward it to postmaster@demon.co.uk, who would then take great pleasure in rendering Hettie's account immediately extinct.

'If you're going to post something more than once, at least make sure you're sending it to people who'll appreciate it. Maybe three or four environmental newsgroups, or people who've subscribed to your "green" mailing lists.'

'Ah,' Hettie said. 'I do vish you had explained zat earlier. See, yesterday I posted my "Stop Deforestation: Criminalise Junk Mail" protest letter to all 14,000 of ze Usenet groups.'

SISTERS UNITE FOR FREEDOM

Hettie's online sisters

Recently Hettie had been Net-surfing big-time – it helped pass the evening hours and the early mornings since Azeem had left her to be a relief worker in India.

An all-night IRC bitching session with Grrrl and Sappho had seen her through it. One of Grrrl's long-term partners (which she called her S>O – 'significant other') had just dumped her too – for an art student at Vancouver University – which Grrrrl found hard to believe:

```
Grrl> i mean Cindi wouldn't recognise a
UNIX _command if it came up and bit her on
the butt. She doesn't even know her own
university email address.

[snip]
```

Bytes
>>> CYBER-HARASSMENT

The Internet may obscure identity, but many women find that the sexual harassment they experience offline frequently follows them online in the form of explicit e-mail and messages.

Juliet Wisner, 21, who met her fiancée online, said she has been harassed, but not enough to discourage her from using the Internet.

'What girl hasn't been harassed online?'

Hettie tries to bring womens' issues into any online discussion and frequently picks up on what she perceives to be sexist attitudes. She is engaged in a protracted e-mail debate with the Sega Corporation, demanding to know why they haven't launched a product called 'GameGirl' – not that she'd buy it if they did because the concept of competitive gaming is against her moral standpoint.

Her ambition is to become MTV's 'webmistress', and she is slowly moving towards her goal by regularly contributing stories like 'Michael Jackson's favourite Web page'.

Her personal home page, 'Sisters Unite For Freedom', is still 'under construction' and has been so for the last six months. So far it contains a picture of Anita Roddick and an enormous 2-Meg sound file of Gloria Gaynor singing 'I Will Survive', which no-one has yet had the patience to download. She reads as many 'zines as she can get hold of and is in the process of setting up her own 'anti-male bastards' Web site called 'No Bollocks'.

```
Wisner observed. 'Everyone I know has had
some form of stalker. It gets annoying, but
all you can do is delete their e-mail and
ignore their messages. It's not like they
know where you live.'
 Women are still very much a minority on
the Net, and that means they get an immense
amount of attention in live chat areas and
also in newsgroups.
 CyberAngels advise women to ignore the
harasser completely, change channels, ask
the harasser politely to leave them alone,
warn they will report the harasser to his or
her service provider, sign off for half an
hour or, as a last resort, change user name
or provider.
```

http://ftp.eff.org/

EMOTIONS

Hettie was very taken by an article in *Internut* magazine about 'Emoticons', which Net-heads use to decorate their text in order to communicate humour, sadness or just plain boredom.

Emoticon directory

:-)	Your basic smile. This smile is used to inflect a sarcastic or joking statement since we can't hear voice inflection over the Internet
:-(	Frownie. Net-head did not like that last statement or is upset or depressed about something
:)	Mini-smilie
:-D	Laughing smilie
:->(-:	Net-head is left-handed
:-@	Net-head is screaming
:-X	Net-head's lips are sealed
;-)	Winky smilie. Net-head has just made a flirtatious or sarcastic remark
>:->	Net-head has just made a devilish remark
>;->	Winky and devil combined. A very lewd remark has just been made
:*)	Net-head is drunk
:'-(	Net-head is crying
[:-)	Net-head is wearing a Walkman
(@:-)	Net-head is wearing a turban
:<)	Net-head went to a private school

Hettie's latest project is to develop a range of 'feminist' smileys, such as:

:-@<	Net-head is pregnant, and
o~:-@<	Net-head is a lesbian but is pregnant thanks to sperm donation

RECYCLING

Hettie's favourite newsgroup is rec.cooking.vegan – but,

however hard she tries, she has been unable to make anything remotely edible (although she does assume this is her fault). She continues to serve her bean-curd concoctions at frequent dinner parties.

Her home is cluttered with useless ethnic trinkets, hand-carved

She was having a few problems with her printer; the guy at Canon customer service had explained – rather tersely, she thought – that frankly, no, he couldn't tell her whether or not the ink in their printer cartridges was obtained from endangered marine species. Hettie is into recycling in a big way. People often commented on her eye-catching earrings made from two

by various tribal groups, which she buys via the Internet ethnic trinkets page. She can't bring herself to throw them away, so she gives them to other people for Christmas and they throw them away instead.

Bored with her unruly ash-blonde hair, she attempted to dye it red with natural henna plant extract. She now has unruly ash-blonde hair with red streaks in it that come out on her organically produced cotton pillow at night.

Late one afternoon, Hettie was trying to resolve the ethical dilemma of whether it would contribute to the deforestation problem if she printed out copies of the Greenpeace Web site.

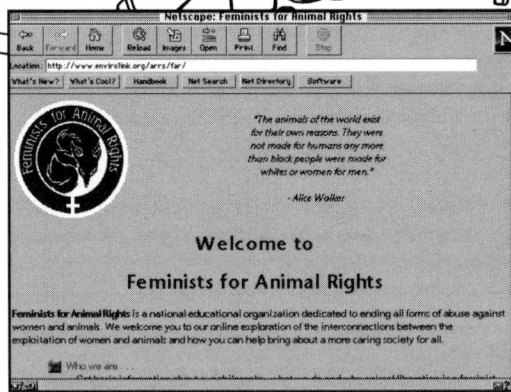

CD-ROMs that came off the cover of a magazine.

She checked out some of the women-only sites on her hotlist – alt.feminists was still clogged up with postings from BigGuy69@aol.com, accusing them all of really being men and suggesting that if they were women they should upload some pictures to prove it. The 'Death To All Male Scumbag B*st*rds!' page had been updated that week, and there were some announcements of new Usenet groups that had just been set up: alt.fan.emily-wolff, alt.fan.emily-wolff.die.die.die and alt.sex.women.domination, although she wasn't sure whether the latter was entirely dedicated to promoting the supremacy of the female gender.

Bytes

>>>BLONDES ON THE OFFENSIVE IN CYBERSPACE

Finnish artist Marita Liulia has created a virtual haven for blondes and other women. Liulia's computer brew of images, sound, text and video mixes lewd jokes and innuendo with the sharp feminist wit of a tough Nordic woman.

Few computer Net-veterans would be drawn by the program's title: 'Ambitious Bitch'. Liulia's ambition is to secure a place for women in anorak-infested cyberspace.

Whether or not you know interactive multimedia, the simplest way to describe 'Ambitious Bitch' is as a sort of computer game with attitude.

http:/www.edita.fi/bitch

HETTI'S FEMINIST LINKS

Confessions of a (nymphomaniac) Cyber-Slut
Erica quotes from Oscar Wilde: 'It is absurd to divide people into good and bad. People are either charming or tedious.'
http://www.sirius.com/~ehall/Welcome.html

Jay's Leftist and 'Progressive' Internet Resources Directory
All the politically correct links you could ever dream of –
even the 'Ability Mall'. Loads of feminist sites.
http://plainfield.bypass.com/~N_E_Research/left.html

Women Leaders On Line Page
'WLO is an organization dedicated to stopping the Radical Right agenda.'
http://worcester.lm.com/women/women.html

Lifestyles
Links to: Feminism and Women's Resources, Feminist Activism, Feminist Majority Foundation – 911 for Women, Women's Health Clinic, Women's Resources Project, and Women's Web.
http://www.freenet.mb.ca/community/lifestyles/index.html

Web Weavers – non-personal pages
'These are the more formal, non-personal pages that women have created.'
http://www.dfw.net/~soulmate/women2.html

Shel's Palace of Fine Girls!!!!
'I don't think that calling myself a "grrrl" or "girl" is derogatory to my person. I am a smart Girl. I am a strong Gurl. I am a feminist GRRRL. And the semantics bore me. I think it is sad that while there are tons of women/girls/female types online, it's alarmingly difficult to find them.' Links to other cool grrls pages, 'zines and resources.
http://www.thenet-usa.com/mag/staff/shel/grrrl.html

The Pheminist Cyber RoadShow – Searchin' Feminism Searchin' Pheminism.
http://www.oeh.uni-linz.ac.at:8001/~lisa/searchin.html

Gender-Related Links
http://nic2.hawaii.edu/~dineh/gender.html

International Women's Web Sites
http://www-unix.umbc.edu/~korenman/wmst/links_intl.html

Database on Women
Including YOKOHAMA WOMEN'S FORUM, Women's Wire and The Feminist Majority Online.

http://www.suehiro.nakano.tokyo.jp/WOM/English/ACCESS/index.html

Virginia Woolf Web
http://130.54.80.49/VW/INDEX.HTML

Women's HomePage Index in The World
http://vcom.suehiro.nakano.tokyo.jp/WOM/Japanese/ACCESS/index.html

Girls can do anything! (e-zine)
http://ernie.bgsu.edu/~ckile/GCDAthree.htm

Amy's Obsessions
E-mail address lists with a women-only policy. Lots of links and info on Web design courses.
http://www.best.com/~agoodloe/home.html

Cybergrrl
http://www.cybergrrl.com/

Femina
http://www.femina.com

Erica Jong embraces a new age
Karen Goldfarb interviews Erica Jong, 25 June 1995.
http://www.sfgate.com/examiner/prev/examiner-062595/STYLE-25697.html

Creating A Celebration of Women Writers
http://www.cs.cmu.edu/Web/People/mmbt/women/celebration.html

Newsgroups
alt.abortion.inequity
alt.censorship
alt.child-support
alt.fan.tank-girl
alt.feminism
alt.music.alternative.female
alt.politics.british
alt.politics.radical-left
alt.save.the.earth
soc.feminism
soc.feminism.resources
soc.women
talk.abortion

Chapter

13

MAKING USE OF THE MEDIUM

Revenge via the Net
Looking for love and Brad Pitt
Top ten stars in Cyberspace
Mr Newbie gets RSI (repetitive strain injury)
Mrs Newbie becomes a MUD Mum
Howard's double identity
Get your female on the e-mail – meeting via the Net

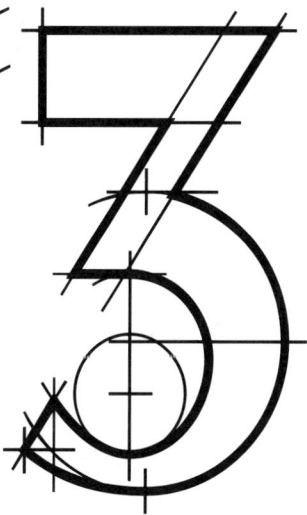

Revenge
via the Net

Hettie leafed through the tattered collection of photos, which were mostly of Azeem batting for the Young Pakistani Eleven. These were her only mementos of their relationship. She particularly treasured the one of him on his back, head resting in the lap of a leather-clad gay. Azeem had claimed to remember nothing about it the next day.

She sat brooding over the episode as she poured the last few drops from the bottle of Hungarian Bull's Blood she had opened half an hour earlier. She logged on to check her e-mail, but no message from Azeem awaited her. This was not suprising as there had been no message since he left four months before. The more she thought about it, the more venomous her feelings towards Azeem became.

Her eye fell again on the collection of photos, and she suddenly had a nasty idea. Two days later she launched the Gay Cricketer page on the World Wide Web. It was a real work of art. A set of little cricket icons at the top of the page. A cap for the star rating – 5 caps was the best mark.

Pride of place was given to the photo of Azeem and his leather-clad companion. But somehow just knowing it was there was not enough. She logged on to alt.sex.bi and left a message telling all the readers of the page where they could find some really cool stuff. She e-mailed Stephen Fry and asked him to make a link from his home page. Once her revenge Web site was up and running, she somehow didn't feel so bad about Azeem any more.

Hettie's day begins around 1:30pm. After watching a daytime soap and making some breakfast, she decides to use the computer her parents bought her for her college work to cruise the Internet. What the hell, she's never going to make it in time for that afternoon lecture anyway.

POLITICALLY CORRECT LIST OF FAVOURITE ACTIVIST SITES

http://www.oneworld.org/oxfam/
The Oxfam site links you to pages and pages of the disturbing truth about what is happening the world.

http://www.greenpeace.org/
Greenpeace Web site – home of the international environment campaigners. Lists ongoing campaigns, highlights areas of concern and asks for money. All links are green and take you to other environmental campaigners as well.

<webmaster@greenpeace.org>

http://www.fund-raising.com/nichenet/frindex.html
The site for the campaigner. Here you can order all sorts of knick-knacks to sell at your jumble sale or fête and find

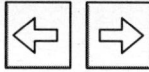

instructions on how to set up your own fund-raising event.
<nichenet@fund-raising.com>

http://www.envirolink.org/arrs/far/
Feminists for animal rights 'FAR' out! A site dedicated to ending the exploitation of animals and women. Posted articles on associated subjects and a 'come and join us page'.
finla001@mc.duke.edu.

http://envirolink.org/arrs/HSA/hsa.html
The Hunt Saboteurs Association. Online info on how to sab any hunt any where, the legal aspects and hunt-sab groups around the UK.

LOOKING FOR *Love*
(and Brad Pitt)

Hettie is soon in love again – only it's unrequited and she's never going to meet him. She spends hours gazing into his eyes and Brad Pitt doesn't even wink back; he doesn't care that his page is top of her bookmarks **(http://www.sils.umich.edu/~cat/pages).**

She tries the Secret E-Mail addresses and home-pages site **(http://www2.islandnet.com/~luree/fanmail.html)** to try and find out how to contact him. After much browsing she finally finds what is allegedly Brad's e-mail address (CIAOBOX@MSN.COM). Now all she needs is something to send him. How about a poem?… Brad seems like a sensitive kind of guy. Hettie tries to come up with something suitable, something that will catch his attention, but she never gets past the first line: 'Oh Brad Pitt, you are so fit'. In desperate need of some good material, Hettie webs over to the 'Beauty and Love in Poetry' site **(http://www.cc.gatech.edu/grads/b/Gary.N.Boone/love_in_poetry.html)**, where some of the world's finest love poems can be found.

Just then she receives an e-mail from France giving her the address of a site containing naked pictures of Brad Pitt! Fingers trembling, she types in the URL, glad she doesn't have to use the college computer where anyone could walk past and discover that she really was a bit of a pervert! She reaches her destination **(http://www.eden.com/~phryday/EJD/bp.html)** and adds the page to her collection of bookmarks.

Hettie is not alone in her obsession with Brad Pitt. He is the most popular male on the Internet.

MR NEWBIE GETS REPETITIVE STRAIN INJURY (RSI)

Mr Newbie had long been an ardent admirer of the work of Tom Clancy, author of *The Hunt for Red October*. That evening Clancy was due to meet his fans in the CompuServe forum GO BOOKPLUG. A few weeks later Michael Moorcock would engage in some online dialogue with his fans.

He logged on at 9.30pm, as instructed by the announcement in his e-mail that morning. Disconsolately, Mr Newbie discovered that the event had been set for 9.30pm alright, but in New York, five hours behind London. Why was it always daytime somewhere in Cyberspace, he wondered, as he began a game of Netropolis on the Delphi Web site to while away the hours.

Five hours later when the great dialogue started in New York Mr Newbie was suffering from an overdose of computer terminal – from muscle tension to soreness and pain, from irregular breathing to eye strain, migraine headaches and sporadic rapid heartbeat. He recognised the symptoms because he had read about them that day in *The Computer User's Survival Guide* by Joan Stigliani (O'Reilly & Associates, Inc., 1995).

Much is made of the advances technology has created in medicine, but repetitive strain injury and the effect it can have on your tendons and nerves is probably the greatest blessing the computer age has bestowed upon the medical profession.

The worst was still to come – in the long term he knew he could expect 'allergies, skin rashes and hives accompanied by dramatic changes in appetite and weight…. ulcers, cancer, and decreased enjoyment of sex'. 'Hang on, though, that could happen even without computers' he realised.

All the same, Joan Stigliani's terrifying tract left him wondering whether his headache was caused by tension or eye strain and whether it was curable or whether he would just have to tolerate it for the rest of his life.

RSI is a risky business; any regular Net-head can get the condition, and for many it may be years before they become aware of the problem. The tendency of keyboards to bring on muscle disorders will be an electronic boon to physiotherapists and acupuncturists everywhere.

Exposure to computer-generated radiation in the office is believed by some doctors to cause miscarriage, cancer, cataracts, skin rash, electromagnetic sensitivity, chronic fatigue syndrome and hearing discomfort, Mr Newbie learned.

'Assistive technology' can help identify the right glasses or lenses or wrist-rests or highbacked chair, but at 3am on a rainy Sunday night assistive technology didn't seem much use to Mr Newbie. He would have felt uncomfortable in any sort of chair.

Spending too much time on a computer may increase the stress the machine can cause. Thought patterns perpetuate stress, which begins in the mind but can be reduced using relaxation techniques.

As the moderator introduced the great author Mr Newbie crept away to bed and counted emoticons until he fell into a deep, dreamless sleep.

MRS NEWBIE BECOMES A MUD MUM

After the men in the house had been on the Net for a few months Mrs Newbie began to have the occasional surf. Pretty soon it was she who became the main addict of the household – staying in all night playing multi-user games was less hassle

Bytes

>>>TOP TEN STARS IN CYBERSPACE

Net-heads are forever searching for their favourite stars in Cyberspace.

They use the Internet 'search engines', which are like the *Yellow Pages* of Cyberspace. Type in a name and the search engine will come back with the relevant Internet address(es).

Infoseek, a major Internet search engine, announced the most popular stars for whom it gets online requests. The top 10 list is a ranking based on the number of recent searches for each celebrity.

than going out and hiring a babysitter.

Multi-user games, known as MUDs, are one of the most interesting things about the Net.

MUDs and MOOs

There are over 700 MUDs and MOOs (an object-oriented MUD, which makes no difference to the actual experience) – some with audiences of up to 40,000, others known to only a few hundred participants. MUD stands for 'Multi-User Dungeon' (or 'Dimension', some say). Until recently they were text-only environments where players created fantasy scenarios. Because many of the players were students, they were likely to create Dungeons and Dragon-type games where they took on characters like Gandalf the Wizard or Queen Mu.

1. Pamela Anderson
2. Cindy Crawford
3. Anna Nicole Smith
4. Jenny McCarthy
5. Brad Pitt
6. Madonna
7. Demi Moore
8. Sharon Stone
9. Patricia Ford
10. Teri Hatcher

Source: http://guide.infoseek.com

USA Today regularly carries a list of stars who are due to make special appearances in Cyberspace.

http://www.usatoday.com/life/cyber/cyber1.htm

But MUDs, MOOs and MUSEs have now been recognised for their potential as environments for collaborative research, education and business. MUDs can be seen as multi-user e-mail, or as Usenet with no time delay. This makes them places where a group of geographically separated people can get things done or agreed quickly.

The biggest and oldest is Lamda MOO, started at Xerox Parc, the photocopier company's advanced research centre. Xerox started it to test out its robots, and to this day the purpose of the game is to tell whether you are talking to a human or a 'bot'.

Because the games are still text-only, most Mud-heads are students or die-hard enthusiasts, but the jump to graphics has started. The first 3-D site where players can take control of graphical figures in a checkerboard landscape is now being tested on the World Wide Web.

The MUDs are already popular locations for business meetings and electronic classrooms. MUDs take place in real-time, they produce a record of conversations, and they are scaleable – meaning that any number of people can take part at the same time. When two players meet in a room they can interact by typing phrases to one another.

It is the capacity for interaction that has taken MUDs from a game to the wider social and business arena. Using the Telnet application, anyone can pay a visit to MediaMOO at telnet://guest@purple-crayon.media.mit.edu:8888 and observe media researchers at work. There are MUD-based educational conferences, where participants show slides, hold up signs or walk around the room. Increasingly, business researchers and teachers are meeting in MUDs. The Telnet application can be used to access any MUD, although MUD-specific applications, called 'clients', are better for this purpose.

Meeting Space Software, from World Benders (wb-info@worldbenders.com), sets up a MUD for business communications. By letting business people create and use MOO at its Internet site, Metaverse (http://io.com/io/metaverse/) rents virtual office space to virtual corporations.

In 1996 AlphaWorld – 'the first fully functioning on-line community' – was launched. Net-heads enter a virtual environment filled with other real people. The software is available on the World's Web site (http://www.worlds.net). Citizens of AlphaWorld have the right to own land and build on it, engage in commerce, explore the environment and experience its content. All these activities take place in a shared space, where citizens from anywhere in the physical world experience the same environment, see the same surroundings and can chat with other Net-heads.

Meanwhile, CompuServe and Fujitsu have unveiled WorldsAway, an animated virtual world for CompuServe members worldwide. WorldsAway is a cyberplace where online users create their own animated representations called 'avatars' and socialise with other users all over the world in a graphical landscape. Members will be able to rent their own virtual apartment, where they can host private gatherings and decorate their space with a variety of in-world objects, including (because the product was launched in December 1995) holiday accessories like wreaths, candles and even a Christmas tree. The game is reached by typing the command GO AWAY from anywhere within CompuServe.

Bert now finds his mum unbelievably embarrassing, particularly when she tries to get his friends to play Doom when they're busy doing their homework. He wishes his parents were embarrassing in a more conventional way – by being hippies or criminals or something – instead of turning up two hours late to collect them from school because she was about to defeat the Forest-Dwelling Warlock with the Flaming Torch and go up another level.

In appearance she's pretty much like any other mum except that in the hairdressers she's the one under the driers who's reading *WIred* and *PC Gamer* instead of *Woman's Realm*.

HOWARD THE GEEK'S OTHER IDENTITY

Howard has a double-identity problem. Despite his sanctimonious attitude towards the Net-foibles of others, in his off-duty moments Howard transforms himself into ridgerider@aol.com.

Howard, in his capacity of Ridge Rider, and Carol – 'Miss Perfect 69' on the IRC – met over the Internet when she posted a comment about Captain Picard of Star Trek and he flamed her about it for six weeks.

They were both tongue-tied when he flew over to London to meet her at the Dukes pub, where Star Trek fans drink on a Saturday night. But, despite the fact that she loved Star Trek and he hated it, they soon found they had a lot in common. As dawn broke they were still arguing endearingly about the merits of Apple Macs vs IBM PCs.

They married six months later. They were, of course, first married on a MUD – he was an Elf and she was a Barbarian Warrior. They both have relatively well-paid jobs, which means they can afford to spend lots of time connected to the Net. They have also been able to afford a house, but they can't move in yet because the walls are being ripped out to install ethernet cable.

Once the builders are finished they will have somewhere to hang their collection of interesting computer-generated abstract art, which gives their guests headaches if they look at it for too long. They also have two video recorders so they can video the things they don't have time to watch because they're too busy surfing the Net. They are always buying the latest labour-saving devices – a cordless desk-mounted negative-ion generator, a thermal pressure-point-stimulating foot-spa for the cat and so forth. They have all sorts of sophisticated telephone-answering machines – devices that actually make it far more difficult for people to communicate with them. They bought a CD-ROM writing device purely in order to be able to send 'multimedia' Christmas cards to their friends, most of whom don't have CD-ROM drives.

When they move house they won't bother to fill in a form at the post office for forwarding because they don't get any snail mail any more – not important snail mail, anyway.

They spend half their life getting frustrated with bits of technical equipment that don't work, which means that both of them suffer from very high stress levels. They are attempting to combat this with a MindMaster Virtual Reality Relaxation Device but, despite hours spent poring over the troubleshooting guide, they still can't get it to function properly.

Their quality time is spent hanging out on IRC and sending letters (by e-mail, of course) to newspapers defending people who use the Net a lot.

They actually like Windows 95. It makes their lives more interesting. They get very annoyed when things aren't simple to use, and their phone number is now on a blacklist at Technical Support. They'd like to be able to talk about programming and share in nerdy jokes, but they just haven't got the time or the motivation to learn any of the relevant information. They do, however, have a copy of *Teach Yourself C++ in 21 Days* in the downstairs toilet and Bill Gates' biography on the coffee table. Sometimes they switch them round.

THE ONLINE REACTIONARY

Hettie is a representative of the predominant activist type on the Net – young, left-wing and into fashionable causes.

But every other interest group in the world is also represented. There are pages for Scientologists, white skinheads, Black Panthers and neo-Nazis.

A British Conservative MP, David Shaw, was the first Member of Parliament to become a Net-head. He caused outrage in the uk.politics newsgroup by posting insulting messages about the Labour Party's leaders.

There were more than a thousand replies to his original message one Sunday in 1994 when he wrote: 'As the knives are sharpened and the discussion gets more heated in the Labour end of the tea room, only a Tory MP can give a balanced assessment of the real issues'. Shaw, who publicly identifies himself as an MP on his journeys through Cyberspace, went on to describe Labour

MPs as 'unbalanced', but it was his assessment of the Shadow Cabinet that caused the most offence, mainly because it was so juvenile... Robin Cook: 'He is nicer than he looks (just)'; Margaret Beckett: 'models herself (and especially her voice) on Margaret Thatcher'; Tony Blair: 'Life has been good for Tony – some of his colleagues think too good'; Gordon Brown: 'Being unmarried might not be a problem, if some of the gossip factory rumours are as untrue as they are in relation to others'; John Prescott: 'The Tory Party Choice'.

'Roll on the General Election when David Shaw gets his come uppance' was one of the politer replies posted in the uk.politics discussion group.

'You are a member of the most repellent, the cruelest [sic], most merciless regime that this country can remember', said another.

Shaw also used the Net to campaign against the fact that government press releases, which can be widely distributed over the Internet, are being sold to a private computer database service, Datastar, yielding the government an annual income of £35,000. Datastar charges £60 per hour to researchers and journalists.

'It is denying the electorate access to free information which is theirs by right' said Shaw, a former merchant banker.

Bytes

>>>LABOUR MEP USES NET TO COUNTER FRAUD

A Euro-MP today launched a Cyberspace war against fraud and waste in the European Union. John Tomlinson is the first Euro-MP with detailed World Wide Web pages, which include an appeal for help against crimes against the EU budget.

The Labour MEP for Birmingham West is making information available on subjects ranging from European grants and animal welfare to this year's intergovernmental conference pages and the fight against fraud.

Tomlinson received his first e-mail message of congratulations from European Transport Commissioner Neil Kinnock. Tomlinson said it was no good relying only on the 40 million-a-year information budget handled by the Brussels Commission.

http://www.poptel.org.uk/john.tomlinson/

Chapter

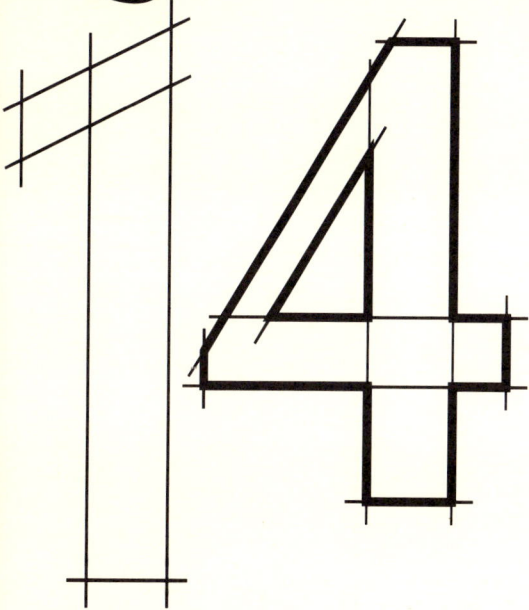

CYBERPUNKS

Malcolm has a secret project to flood the Internet with World music. Then his genius will be recognised. He is working on software that will compress music into tiny files so that entire singles can be sent down the Net in seconds. His plan is to undermine the power structure of the existing record industry. So he has to be very, *very* secretive because if the Industry discovered his plan they would kill him for sure.

Malcolm works long hours into the night on the software, which is almost ready. It has been 'almost ready' for about two years. His friend Robert Lord, 24, is founder and 'President' of the Internet Underground Music Archive (IUMA), which exists to give away music by unknown bands via the Net. Because they are non-commercial the record companies are worried about them.

'We are not retailers,' said Lord when he launched the IUMA server in Wood Green, London. 'We are a place in Cyberspace where musicians can meet their listeners with as few intermediaries as possible.'

On the first Friday of each month at 7pm, next to the virtual reality machines at the Trocadero in London's Piccadilly Circus, Malcolm and a nervous collection of fellow Cyberpunks gather, wondering whether this will be the moment when they are busted for their years of hacking – breaking into distant computers via the telephone system. Malcolm lives in a grungy house in Wales. He has come to London with a couple of pals – The Red Dwarf and Hackattack – for an F2F with the faces behind the keyboards he meets on the Internet chat channels in the middle of the night.

Hacking is the best and the worst of Internet culture. At times it is just innocent exploration, the digital generation flexing its intellectual muscles. But it can also be simple criminality – stealing money by cracking passwords to enter a bank or other big company computer. It is not specific to the Internet, but the bands of hackers, who know each other sometimes only by pseudonyms, spend hours on the Internet talking to each other and using the info-hiway to attempt to break into computers.

At the Trocadero they talk about the latest computers they have targeted and swap lists of incompetent sysops, the Geeks who defend computers against intruders and monitor for warning signs, like unexplained use of the CPU (central processing unit). They tell tales of searches through the paper waste outside the offices of multinationals and swap phone-card access codes. After an hour the group has assembled and they move on to a secret location. They are still talking about 'source codes', or the latest PC clones, or ways of reprogramming the chip inside mobile phones.

The Cyberpunks are the anarchists of the Internet. They are as technically competent as the Geeks but believe that the Net is for anybody to do anything with. The Geeks are their natural enemies. Where the Geeks want order and control, the Cyberpunks want anarchy. To their chagrin, the Cyberpunks have most in common with the Net-profiteers, who would also like to see the Net continue as a system of controlled anarchy.

FAVOURITE CYBERPUNK SITES

http://www.cs.uidaho.edu/lal/cyberspace/cyberpunk/cyberpunk.html

If you're not a Cyberpunk and don't know what one is, you can find out beneath the grafitti-sprayed wall. Links to cyberbooks, including Willian Gibson's *Neuromancer*, one of the best books about Cyberpunks ever written.
<sheneman@cs.uidaho.edu

http://www.wwmatrix.com/cyberpunk/index.m.html

Boing Boing, the unofficial cyberpunk home page. Beneath an electronic circuit board you can link from cyberpunk movies (*Clockwork orange*, *Brazil* and *Blade runner*) to cyberpunk games (the Cyberpunk Experiment, a free-for-all Internet game by e-mail) to a list of cyberpunk magazines.
vanzoest@mailhost.net

http://146.19.2.3/~alquier/cyber.html

Oo la la, a fantastic site from Europe (and a Magellan four star). Truly interactive within the site (not just links to like sites), and no end of cool cybergraphics.
alquier@eerie.eerie.fr

http://www.en.utexas.edu/~tonya/cyberpunk/

This site about cyberspace and cyberculture is presented by students of the University of Texas, Austin, home town of Bruce Sterling.

http:www.hallucinet.com/retailslut/

A spoof retail page, which also takes off sex on the Net

PGP – THE CYBERPUNK CODE

Malcolm's other hobby is breaking into top-secret defence computers – just to prove it can be done. He is not interested in money except to pay his massive phone bills, and he is negotiating with a journalist so that when he finds that elusive big story he will be able to sell it fast and for a good price.

He is dating a secretary at Alcatel, a French electronics conglomerate. She is smart but, exasperatingly, she is not interested in hacking. In a way that is a good thing. She tells him the passwords for the French defence project she is working on because she thinks they are so funny. Ultimately, however, it is a bad thing because it means that he can't give her his PGP key, which is the hacker's equivalent of a front-door key.

PGP is short for Pretty Good Privacy, and although PGP is not perfectly secure it is pretty good – good enough for the government to have banned it in the US. It is used to send encrypted messages on the Internet. Even if someone is spying on the transmissions, there would be nothing they could do without the private PGP key. Every hacker has two PGP keys, each of which consists of a string of letters and numbers. The public key allows others to encode messages and send them to the owner. Then the private key is used to 'unlock' the messages at the other end. PGP is freely available for downloading from dozens of Internet sites.

Cyberpunks spend a lot of time inside the bowels of computers which they have liberated from big companies. They like to travel with heavy cases packed with comms equipment, which they can assemble in record time and run direct from a hotel main switchboard without the management being aware of its existence.

The two sides of the Cyberpunk – the explorer and the looter – were explored in the movie *Hackers*, which was shot on location in the UK. Companies from Jolt Cola to Apple Computer paid for the right to have their products shown on screen. Iain Softley, the film's director and executive producer, says there is a 'dark side' to hacking but the typical hacker is only 'mildly subversive'. Softley sees parallels between the sixties psychedelic generation and the current 'cyberculture' that is emerging in music, fashion and the club scene.

Like all youth cultures, hackers are 'breaking society's rules as an expression of freedom and character', says Softley. But the difference is that the rules are still being made in this new and evolving area.

Bytes

>>>TRANS-PACIFIC INTERNET PRANK

A 14-year-old Australian Internet surfer triggered a trans-Pacific police operation when a prank backfired, said a police spokesman.

Inspector Richard Lane said the schoolboy sent messages via the Internet to the United States claiming he was a 26-year-old man with a gun who was about to commit suicide.

After police in Redmond in Washington state contacted police in Western Australia the forces on both sides of the Pacific spent several hours trying to track down the suicidal Internet surfer. When Perth police finally identified the source of the messages, the youngster was still typing away on his personal computer at his parents' home.

Although there is a charge of creating a false belief, the boy's parents have assured the police that they can deal with the situation. They were not too pleased to find the police on their doorstep at 3:30 a.m.

The basic coin of their transactions are passwords, phone numbers and security codes.

'Hacking into a public access computer, like a Hospital or a University, that's really lame,' I was told at the Trocadero Centre. 'CompuServe, Delphi, where you get five free hours to find another password, that's easy.' Unix isn't much harder. 'It was never designed to be a secure system. They've learnt to lock the front door now, but left the back window open … It only gets interesting after Unix.'

The guys who were telling me this had Net-names like Veghead or Aceeed. Away from their keyboards they look like the stagehands who set up the equipment at rock concerts.

They are not particularly wise or worldly or mature. Some of them will never grow up. Some will grow up to be corporate data security consultants, and some will be criminals.

I asked them whether, in a skill so important to the future of the country, there should be special schools for people who are caught hacking. They thought that was hilarious. 'Yes, if you're caught,' said Otaku, 'you need a school.'

THE CYBERPUNK KIT

Like Otaku, most Cyberpunks carry big, heavy shoulder bags, which are worth further examination. Unzip one of these cyber-bags and here are the typical contents:

Laptop UNIX workstation – UNIX is the language used by mainframe computers, which are the cornerstone of the Internet. The laptop was self-built to the user's own design using a 486 motherboard lifted from a computer at his boring day job, where the eviscerated computer is still standing idle despite attempts by the IT department to resuscitate it. No one has yet thought of checking to see if the motherboard is still there.

Multimeter – An essential piece of low-tech gear, used to wire the laptop direct into a phone line or while turning a pay-phone into a free world dialler.

Gusto – The first mass-market smart drug.

Neuromancer, by William Gibson – This is the book they all rave about, and some have actually read it. *Snow Crash* and *Hacker Crackdown* are acceptable alternatives.

LAPTOP
UNIX
MACHINE

MEMO PAD
BOUND WITH
PRINTED
CIRCUIT BOARD

COPY OF
JOHNNY
MNEMONIC

2600
MAGAZINE

VOLTMETER

LOTS OF
JUNK FOOD:
COCA-COLA,
CHEERIOS,
NACHOS,
CHINESE
TAKEAWAYS

PIZZA

CHINESE

JOHNNY MNEMONIC

2600

PARNETER

PIZZA

PAGER

HEAVY BAG
FULL OF
CABLES

HOME-MADE
MODEM

A cellular phone – This is spelt 'fone' and has a cloned chip, allowing unlimited free calls.

Dozens of leads and cables – Essential for connecting anything to just about anything else.

CYBERPUNK BOOKS

Neuromancer, *Count Zero* and *Mona Lisa Overdrive*, by William Gibson
   The 'Cyberspace Trilogy'.
Mirrorshades the Cyberpunk Anthology Bruce Sterling ed.

Useful pointer to actual no-kidding Movement Cyberpunks.
Mindplayers, by Pat Cadigan
   Her best novel. An absolute must-have.
Heatseeker, by John Shirley
   Shirley's short stories. His most significant and influential work.
Deserted Cities of the Heart, by Lewis Shiner
   Shiner's best SF novel.
Slam, by Lewis Shiner
   Intriguing cyberpunk mainstream non-genre novel.
Software and *Wetware*, by Rudy Rucker

Best-known novels of deranged math professor/hacker/cyberpunk.

Transreal, by Rudy Rucker
>   Every short piece Rucker ever wrote. Enormous. Like being hit on the head with a bowling ball.

Blood Music, by Greg Bear
>   Bear's most c-wordish book.

Crystal Express, by Bruce Sterling
>   Sterling's short work.

Schismatrix, by Bruce Sterling
>   Post-human space opera.

Islands in the Net, by Bruce Sterling
>   21st-century global information politics.

The Difference Engine, by William Gibson and Bruce Sterling
>   19th-century cyberpunk by subgenre's foremost critics' darlings.

Other Useful Fiction:

Virtual Light, by William Gibson
>   A new, more intimate view of the future by the gomi-no-sensei.

Halo, by Tom Maddox
>   Remarkable SF treatment of robots and artificial intelligence.

Globalhead, by Bruce Sterling
>   Sterling's second story collection.

Patterns, by Pat Cadigan
>   Cadigan's short work. Great range of topics and treatments.

Synners, by Pat Cadigan
>   Cadigan's well-received second novel.

Frontera, by Lewis Shiner
>   Shiner's first novel, about mission to Mars.

Look into the Sun, by James Patrick Kelly
>   Interesting novel by peripheral cyberpunk.

Arachne, by Lisa Mason
>   Cyberspace robots vs drug-addict San Francisco lawyer-careerists. Weirdissimo.

Snow Crash, by Neal Stephenson
>   Fine example of second-generation cyberpunk by Seattle hacker.

Hardwired, by Walter Jon Williams
>   Williams' most successful effort.

Spacetime Donuts and **White Light**, by Rudy Rucker
>   Rucker's early novels. Brilliantly deranged.

Involution Ocean and **The Artificial Kid**, by Bruce Sterling
>   Sterling's first two novels. SF adventures.

Semiotext(E) SF Rudy Rucker, Peter Lamborn Wilson and Robert Anton Wilson, eds.
>   Story anthology of bad craziness. Quite likely to cause protests from scandalized parents and censors.

Magazines:

MONDO 2000
>   'Cyberpunk' as glossy West Coast fashion magazine. It Had To Happen.

bOING bOING
>   Ultra-happening cyberslacker antizine from the heart of digitized desktop bohemia.

Isaac Asimov's Science Fiction Magazine
>   Least reactionary of the standard American SF magazines.

Interzone

Foremost British SF magazine. Libraries should carry this worthy 'zine as a public service.

Science Fiction Eye
More-or-less official lit-crit organ of cyberpunk SF and assorted fellow-travellers. Like most fanzines, sadly sporadic.

Science Fiction Studies
Dull, grey, academic rag seized in startling coup by wacky post-modernists. Now almost readable!

Wired
The first magazine of the 1990s that actually looks and acts like it belongs in this decade.

Non-Fiction, Critical Studies:

Storming the Reality Studio Larry McCaffery ed.
Cyberpunk's man-in-academe gives his highly postmodern take on matters in this bug-crusher anthology.

Cyberpunk: Outlaws and Hackers on the Computer Frontier, by Katie Hafner and John Markoff
The best book to date on the outlaw 'computer underground'.

Across the Wounded Galaxies Larry McCaffery ed.
McCaffery interviews various weirdo leading-lights of porno SF, including Gibson and Sterling.

The Hacker Crackdown: Law and Disorder on the Computer Frontier, by Bruce Sterling
It's not just for breakfast any more.

Terminal Identity, by Scott Bukatman
Headlong foray across the wild terrain of postmodern technology theory.

LIST OF UNDERGROUND HACKER/CYBERPUNK GROUPS

```
The Administration \ Advanced
Telecommunications, Inc. (ATI) \ ALIAS \
American Tone Travelers \ Anarchy Inc. \
Apple Mafia \ The Association \ Atlantic
Pirates Guild (APG)
   Bad Ass Mother Fuckers (BAMF) \ Bellcore
\ Bell Shock Force (BSF) \ Black Bag
   Camorra \ C&M Productions \ Catholics
Anonymous \ Chaos Computer Club \ Chief
Executive Officers (CEO) \ Circle Of Death \
Circle Of Deneb \ Club X \ Coalition of
Hi-Tech Pirates (CHP) \ Coast-To-Coast \
Corrupt Computing \ Cult Of The Dead Cow
(-cDc-) \ Custom Retaliations
   Damage Inc. \ D&B Communications \ The
Dange Gang \ Dec Hunters \ Digital Gang (DG)
\ DPAK
   Eastern Alliance \ The Elite Hackers Guild
\ Elite Phreakers and Hackers Club \ The
Elite Society Of America \ EPG \ Executives
Of Crime \ Extasyy (Elite)
   Fargo 4A \ Farmers Of Doom (FOD) \ The
Federation \ Feds R Us \ First Class \ Five
O \ Five Star \ Force Hackers \ The 414s
   Hack-A-Trip \ Hackers Of America (HOA) \
High Mountain Hackers \ High Society \ The
Hitchhikers
   IBM Syndicate \ The Ice Pirates \
Imperial Warlords \ Inner Circle \ Inner
Circle II \ Insanity Inc. \ International
Computer Underground Bandits (ICUB)
   Justice League of America (JLA) \ Kaos
Inc. \ Knights Of Shadow (KOS) \ Knights Of
The Round Table (KOTRT)
```

League Of Adepts (LOA) \ Legion Of Doom (LOD) \ Legion Of Hackers (LOH) \ Lords Of Chaos \ Lunatic Labs, Unlimited

Master Hackers \ MAD! \ The Marauders \ MD/PhD \ Metal Communications, Inc. (MCI) \ MetalliBashers, Inc. (MBI) \ Metro Communications \ Midwest Pirates Guild (MPG)

NASA Elite \ The NATO Association \ Neon Knights \ Nihilist Order

Order Of The Rose \ OSS

Pacific Pirates Guild (PPG) \ Phantom Access Associates \ PHido PHreaks \ Phlash \ PhoneLine Phantoms (PLP) \ Phone Phreakers Of America (PPOA) \ Phortune 500 (P500) \ Phreak Hack Delinquents \ Phreak Hack Destroyers \ Phreakers, Hackers, And Laundromat Employees Gang (PHALSE Gang) \ Phreaks Against Geeks (PAG) \ Phreaks Against Phreaks Against Geeks (PAP) \ Phreaks and Hackers of America \ Phreaks Anonymous World Wide (PAWW) \ Project Genesis \ The Punk Mafia (TPM)

The Racketeers \ Red Dawn Text Files (RDTF) \ Roscoe Gang

SABRE \ Secret Circle of Pirates (SCP) \ Secret Service \ 707 Club \ Shadow Brotherhood \ Sharp Inc. \ 65C02 Elite \ Spectral Force \ Star League \ Stowaways \ Strata-Crackers \ The Phrim

Team Hackers '86 \ Team Hackers '87 \ TeleComputist Newsletter Staff \ Tribunal Of Knowledge (TOK) \ Triple Entente \ Turn Over And Die Syndrome (TOADS)

300 Club \ 1200 Club \ 2300 Club \ 2600 Club \ 2601 Club \ 2AF

Ware Brigade \ The Warelords \ WASP

The United Soft WareZ Force (TuSwF) \ United Technical Underground (UTU)

TOP TEN WAYS TO TELL A...
CYBERPUNK GROUPIE

10. Has hair of more than three different (unnatural) colours

9. Her friends all have anonymous email addresses (@anon.penet.fi)

8. Likes 'underground' bands, but only before they become fashionable

7. Owns autographed copies of all Douglas Coupland's novels

6. Types in a mixture of upper and lower case letters

5. Hangs around cybercafes a lot, sipping drinks with names like 'Mind Bomb'

4. Her chat-up lines include 'Are you on the hack/freak scene'?

3. Keeps getting banned from the hackers channel on IRC

2. Stops talking to people after discovering they don't have their own Web site

1. Reads *2600 Magazine* conspicuously on the tube

Sara's American but taking a year off to bum across Europe. She hangs round university computer science departments in the hope of meeting British cyberpunks. She always claims to use a faked credit card number but actually just has a very large bill on her Barclaycard.

She uses anonymous remailers all the time – not because she's worried about being 'busted by the Feds' but because she has an AOL address and doesn't want anyone to find out.

She casually leaves copies of *2600 Magazine* sticking out of her handbag. She knows that British hackers are desperate to get

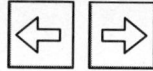

their hands on American copies of *2600 Magazine* and might therefore go to bed with her. Unfortunately, the locals are more impressed by her tongue stud.

She thinks Cyberpunks are great because they're really intelligent. She just wishes they wouldn't talk about computers all the time. She had a brief e-mail flirtation with Norbert after seeing one of his postings about C coding and assuming he was a Cyberpunk, but when she discovered that he was a married bald bloke pushing 40 she stopped writing to him.

She posts to some of the more anarchic IRC groups under the anonymous handle 'Crypto-Babe', but she hasn't yet figured out how to stop the software displaying her genuine e-mail address as well. This means she gets flamed a lot.

Her most prized possession is a T-shirt with an illegal military encryption algorithm printed on it. She got it from a guy in California with whom she had a CU-SeeMe affair. It doesn't fit and she doesn't understand what an encryption algorithm is for, but she's still really proud of it.

Although she claims to be radical and subversive and a feminist, she is desperate to get her photo on 'Babes On The Web'. She's mailed the URL to Rob Toups several times under several different aliases, asking him to 'check out this kewl site'.

She turned up at a hackers' meet wearing a tight T-shirt with her e-mail address on it, hoping people would ask to write it down and then stare at her chest. Annoyingly, they just kept asking her for her list of Warez sites.

Britain is a big disappointment to her. She ends up spending all her time in cybercafes talking to people from the States.

She's trying to write her own cyberpunk novel about how great it is being part of the subversive techno-culture, but keeps

downloading viruses onto her hard disk that wipe out all the text files.

Her current boyfriend is a guy from Holland called Uls who prefers people to use his nickname, dA KiLLeR. He's a programmer who has five different 'cracking' groups interested

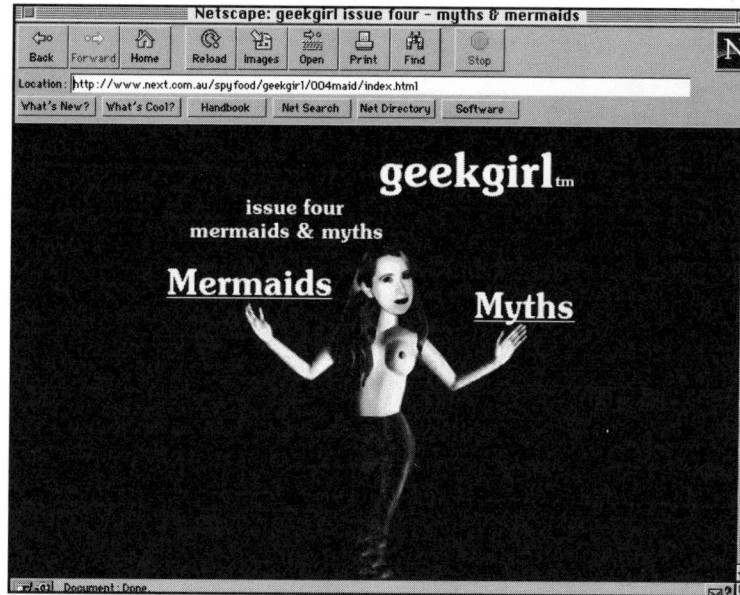

in employing his services. Not only is he tall and blond but he also has lots of money from doing Internet consultancy work for a TV company in Soho (an income which he subsidises by stealing RAM chips and selling them back to the TV company).

Chapter

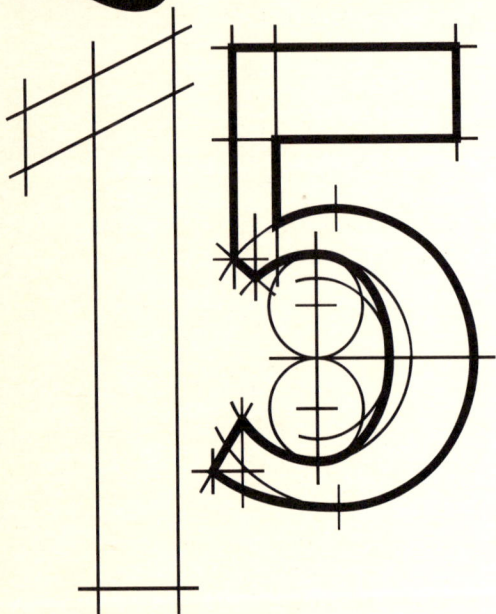

15

SEX ON THE NET

MR NEWBIE INVESTIGATES SEX

Mr Newbie opened the *News of the World* and turned to his favourite page.

```
'Dear Deidre,' began the week's prize-
winning letter, 'I used to think my
relationship was exciting, then I started
reading USENET. Is it still 'being
unfaithful' if I have an affair in
cyberspace?
  J. Nerd-Porter (address witheld)'
```

The letter coincided with the launch of *The News of the World in Cyberspace* on the Rupert Murdoch Net, and Mr Newbie realised he would not need to buy the printed version any more. But it was not the same, he felt. There was no substitute for the walk down to the newsagent and the huge headlines. Still, he decided to try it for a while and see if he got used to it.

The Internet may have been started as part of the plan to build an indestructible communications network, but it has become, among other things, an indestructible global pornography network.

The huge corporate budgets for research into future technologies like virtual reality, CD-ROMs and Internet shopping, banking and edutainment have, sometimes unintentionally, produced very interesting new ways of delivering Cybersex. The technologies are not yet all working in unison, but the human orgasm is already only a computer keystroke away.

Now that the technology is in the hands of the pornographers, they are busy calculating how to cash in on it. The sheer number of people who sit in front of a computer at work every day means there is every reason why the delivery of computer sex should be one of the biggest growth industries of the late 90s.

The BT Advanced Research division in Ipswich is one of many organisations that are unwittingly contributing to the development of Cybersex. The division's research on remote tactile transfer is one example. 'One day we'll be able to transfer all five senses' says Peter Cochrane, the head of advanced research. 'We've already got sight and sound. Touch will be next. Smell and taste will be more difficult, but we'll get there.'

With each new development in the Internet come new ways of doing sex. At first it was mainly confined to the Usenet groups with names like alt.bondage and soc.culture.polyamory. The text-only areas are still the most popular among women interested in sex. They find words more erotic than pictures. By 1995, 18 of the 30 most popular Usenet groups were sex-related. When Delft University allowed porn on its Internet server, traffic increased 900% and the rest of the computer system ground to a halt. They were forced to reverse their decision.

VANESSA AND CHARLES BEGIN AN E-MAIL RELATIONSHIP

For a minority interest group, there was a surprising amount of traffic in soc.culture.indian.kerala.

```
Help! Communication problem (was re: 300
baud modem) (4 messages)
Help! Communication problem (was re: Strict
father) (20 messages)
SPECIAL OFFER: Hard-Polished Indian
Fertility Symbol $10 (5 messages)
Arranged marriages, right or wrong? (13
messages)
Complete History of Keralite Culture **LONG
POSTING** (1/57) (1 message)
Is there a God? (439 messages)
Suggestion - new group
alt.religion.god.dunno (3 messages)
**Arrange your daughter's marriage via
Internet - simply fill in form!** (2
messages)
Horny NY babe wants to go for an Indian ;-)
(1 message)
Internet: work of the Devil? (4 messages)
Allah joke!!!! (10 messages)
```

Fatwa on AOL users? (was re: Allah joke!!!!)
(14 messages)
Merry Christmas (1 message)
Merry Christmas - apology for inappropriate
posting (1 message)

Vanessa scanned the messages without much interest. She'd
started reading this group during her 'ethnic' phase, having
experienced an uncharacteristic pang of guilt while downloading
some pictures of starving black children on the Christian Aid
home page. Vanessa's ethnic phase consisted largely of buying a
mouse mat with a picture of an elephant on it and only sleeping
with men from minority cultures, but at least it eased her
conscience – and rice wine was certainly a lot more potent than
Thunderbird.

She was about to unsubscribe from soc.culture.indian.kerala
when one message caught her eye.

Re: Developing a developing nation
From: cptrickster@pobox.com

Dear Internet Colleague,

By reading this posting, you have taken the
first step towards owning a holiday home
beyond even your wildest speculations.

My company is delighted to be able to offer
this unique purchase opportunity exclusively
to Internet subscribers. Little India is a
brand new private development of timeshare
apartments situated in the picturesque
Ganges delta - a sun-kissed holiday
destination with one of the least serious
rates of malaria and cholera-related
mortality in the Indian sub-continent. The
complex is due to be completed in October
1998 but despite disputes with the local
natives, Trickster Holdings Plc are already
accepting deposits from interested parties.
For a full colour brochure complete with

artist's impression, price list and
vaccination advice, please email me
IMMEDIATELY.

India - Land Of Your Dreams. Can you afford
to pass up this once-in-a-lifetime
opportunity?

Regards,

Charles Trickster
Managing Director, Trickster Holdings Plc

Vanessa contemplated this. It did sound like some sort of
utopian idyll – but obviously the Indian sub-continent had a few
major disadvantages. The endemic outbreaks of dysentery,
occasional unprovoked murders of Western settlers and, most
disturbingly, the unavailability of a local Demon POP.

She checked her mail to see if there were any interesting
messages waiting, which there weren't, so she replied to the
timeshare posting anyway.

To: cptrickster@pobox.com
From: vanessa@blonde.demon.co.uk
Re: Timeshare Development

Hi.

I saw your posting in
soc.culture.india.kerala regarding timeshare
apartments in the Ganges delta.

It has always been my ambition to lie naked
on a sun-drenched Eastern shore, sipping a
long glass of whatever it is they drink out
there and letting the warm water lap softly
over my lithe tanned body - caressing my
smooth skin, whilst my long blonde hair
tumbles in lustrous waves down my bronzed
back and the elephants (NB elephants not
really appropriate, but unsure as to what

other animals are native to India) frolic and gambol around my slim naked body.

Please send me a brochure.

Looking forward to hearing from you.

Vanessa Fox.

She double-clicked her message into the void and thought no more about it.

HETTIE'S ON-LINE RELATIONSHIP

Hettie felt a slight rush of blood on finding another love-mail from Angela. They had met via the alt.fan.tankgirl newsgroup in the earliest of her netsurfing days. She had been, as she put it to herself, exploring her sexuality. It was somehow automatic that the first thing she would do when she had finally mastered the technology was go straight to the sex discussion groups, and after a short exchange in alt.fetish.feet with a woman who turned out to be a man, she had retreated to the safety of alt.wimmin, where the convenor claimed through a combination of intuition and close textual analysis to be able to detect imposters.

She began an e-mail relationship with Angela after spotting her posting about men-who-never-grow-up. Their shared distaste for men-as-boys had blossomed into a mutual admiration that threatened to become an affair had Hettie not refused several offers of meetings, dinners and parties.

Like Hettie, Angela sees the Net as a way to air radical viewpoints. Together they publish home pages with titles like Naked Slut so blokes will find them via the search engines and download their female supremacist tracts.

Hettie is furious that the Net has been dominated by men and sees this as some sort of conspiracy rather than concluding that maybe a lot of women aren't actually that interested in the Internet. She tries to organise mailing lists/chat sessions for like-minded cyberfeminists, but doesn't realise that the majority of

the participants are actually blokes who just fancy having a laugh at her.

When she turned up at a campus hackers' meeting the guys kept asking whose girlfriend she was, so she retaliated by fatally crashing their machines.

She's not actually all that keen on William Gibson's novels, but she feels compelled to read them because Jackie Collins' books don't really have the same cred. Her darkest secret is that she once posted a personal ad to one of the online dating services.

VANESSA'S NIGHT WITH THE NEW MEDIA ELITE

Vanessa lurched blearily back into her office at 2.15am, her head throbbing and her legs more unstable than a 386 PC running Windows 95 on 4 Meg of RAM. She had, for once, been out for the evening. She'd been at a Press launch for the new mass-market Internet service, Britain Online – a glitzy, champagne-swilling bash at which the managing director had announced his intention that 'by the year 2000, sixty percent of the UK's computer users will have run up huge phone bills as a result.'

Fortified by alcohol, a 'lift and separate' Wonderbra and a trowel-full of makeup, Vanessa had spent the entire evening trying to cop off with the editor of *Internut*, one of the country's leading Internet magazines. *Internut*'s editor was not impressed by her chat-up line 'Is that a Psion in your pocket, or are you just pleased to see me?' – partly because it was a Psion pocket PC in his pocket, but mostly because he wasn't remotely pleased to see Vanessa and wished she'd stop trying to sit on his knee. He sloped off at 11pm to get the train back to Leicester and review a new CD-ROM.

Vanessa was more than a little upset. Even playing hard-to-get hadn't got her anywhere. She stumbled through to the kitchen to make herself a cup of strong black coffee.

The percolator gave its normal, authentic rendition of an elderly asthmatic's dying wheezes and dispensed half a cup of what looked and tasted like warm mud. Knocking it back in one, things began to drift into focus. Vanessa wished that some of them would go back to being hazy, drink-distorted semi-

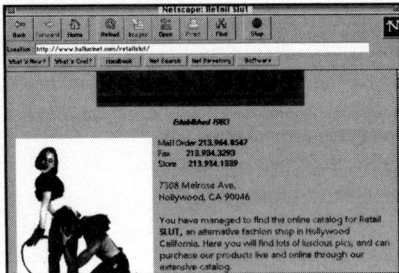

recollections since they were far too humiliating to think about with any degree of clarity. Feeling a sudden need for the comforting anonymity of the Internet, she

slumped down in front of the screen.

DRUNK IN CHARGE OF A MODEM

```
Login: lothips
Password: ******
Invalid login.

Login: lopshit
Password: ******
Invalid login.

Login: hotlips
Password: ******
Login accepted. Welcome, hotlips.
```

Only three attempts to type in her own name – that was pretty good going. She checked the e-mail. A couple of flames, which she zapped into oblivion with a satisfying 'glurp' sound. Something defaming the new release of 'Netscrape' Navigator, three invoices from online shopping services and a brief but nevertheless appallingly mispelled note from Hot2Lips@aol.com offering 'steamy 3-wway action with seXXXy Girlz, emial for details'. Junk mail – all of it. Except for one other message that caught her eye.

```
Trickster Holdings Plc Re: Please contact
me!
```

She perked up a little, downed another cup of silt and read the message with some apprehension.

```
To: vanessa@blonde.demon.co.uk ('Vanessa
Fox')
From: cptrickster@pox.com ('Trickster
Holdings Plc')
Re: Please contact me!

Dear Vanessa,
Thankyou so much for your kind response to
my USENET posting.
Settling in India has also been one of my
fantasies for longer than I care to
remember (oops - showing my age there!).
It's so inspiring - encouraging - to hear
from somebody who shares my vision of the
future.

I will gladly pay your expenses for you to
visit the Little India timeshare complex
site and see our dream become reality.

Do please get in touch. I am totally
serious.

Charles.

Ps. I hope this reaches you intact - I am
sending it from 30,000 feet on board an Air
India flight and e?ffwqwe#fg eriogvqenhio#
sorry, stewardess knocked a croissant into
my Powerbook... Oh, apparently passengers
are forbidden from using mobile phones
during the flight.
```

Vanessa was never one to pass up the opportunity for a freebie. Even blagged CD-ROMs could be put to gainful employment as shoulder pads – a trip to India was definitely a step up from that. Besides, there were the duty-frees to consider.

```
To: cptrickster@pox.com ('Trickster Holdings
Plc')
From: vanessa@blonde.demon.co.uk ('Vanessa
Fox')
Re: Please contact me!

Dear Charles,

Can I call you Charlie? Or maybe Chas or
Chuck?

You sound lovely. I would be delighted to
accept your offer. Let's talk when you
arrive back in the UK.
Yours,

Vanessa. xxx
```

She chewed thoughtfully on the end of a biro until she realised it was the wrong end and was wiping smears of blue ink across her already well-smudged lipstick. Trickster sounded like a guy with style. Panache. How else could she convey that brand of sophisticated dignity which she felt sure he would appreciate in a woman? She paused for a few moments, then added:

```
ps. Hope you get this, I am sending it via
my portable satellite transmitter from the
Piccadilly line train to Cockfosters.
```

DARLING I TOLD YOU NOT TO CALL ME AT THE OFFICE

CHARLES AND VANESSA NEARLY 'GET OFF' VIA E-MAIL

The following day was a Sunday. Vanessa spent the morning engaged in her traditional Sabbath pursuit: scanning the DejaNews Usenet search engine for the keywords 'hangover AND cure'. The search proved relatively fruitless.

```
++GUARANTEED HANGOVER CURE+++
rec.food.drink.beer
Re: Drink Lots Of Water
alt.support.alcohol
Re: Tequila, Brown Sauce and Custard
uk.misc
GUARANTEED HANGOVER CURE didnt work :-(
rec.food.drink.beer
Try this - ice cold lake dive at 6am
rec.sports.scuba
I Nnedd a hnagvoreR crue (9uGRENT!)
alt.fan.vodka
Re: Heavy Drink Problem - advice?
soc.singles
Pan Galactic Gargle Blaster
alt.fan.douglas-adams
How To Avoid Hangover (GUARANTEED!)
alt.teetotallers
Choking on own vomit?
uk.medical
cHOking on someonE else's vomit?
alt.sex.bizarre
Re: Black Coffee
alt.support.caffeine
```

She was in the kitchen when the distinctive You've-Got-Mail 'Ping' drifted through from the office.

```
To: vanessa@blonde.demon.co.uk ('Vanessa
Fox')
From: cptrickster@pox.com ('Trickster
Holdings Plc')
Re: Please contact me!
```

My dear Vanessa,

Many, many thanks for responding so quickly. We must, indeed, speak soon - face to face, instead of letting our fingers do the talking.

I'm sure we have so much in common - not just our mutual love of exotic places. Let me tell you a bit about myself. I am 47, recently single (long story!) and as you know, Managing Director of Trickster Holdings Plc. I am based in Bermuda, London, Tokyo and Madrid, although I have a small place in the States as well (I believe it is called San Francisco - JOKE BTW! So far anyway! ;-)). Physically I am tall, tanned and have dark hair (all my own - almost!). I enjoy the finer things in life - gourmet food, vintage wine and the company of beautiful women. Preferably all at the same time. '-)

Enough of me - tell me about *yourself*. I am dying to know all about you.

Write soon.

;-) Charlie

Her fingers were shaking (partly from excitement, mainly from the caffeine O/D) as she clicked 'Reply' and began stabbing at the keyboard. Despite nurturing an addiction to the Net, Vanessa had never mastered the art of touch typing – particularly when she was in a hurry. Several of her late-night Usenet postings had been cross-posted to soc.lang.esperanto, where they'd circulated for months, defying all attempts at translation.

To: cptrickster@pox.com ('Trickster Holdings Plc')
From: vanessa@blonde.demon.co.uk ('Vanessa Fox')

Re: Please contact me!

dear Charlie

>I enjoy the finer things in life - gourmet food, vintage wine and
>the company of beautiful women. Preferably all at the same time. '-)

its so rare to emetet a real gentleman on tnhe inetnet but it seems that you reaally respopect woenm. Id olove to talk furhtrer with you.

byf ace to aface I presume you mena IRC? Mmet me on chanerel #vanessa tongith at 11pm if uou get this in time. Ill be waiting! Im sure I will enjoy your company (and I dont mena Trickster Holdnings Plc!)

Lov,

Vanessa xxx

NETIQUETTE...
VANESSA: DON'T POST BINARIES TO NON-BINARIES GROUPS

Norbert moved the collection of empty wine bottles off Vanessa's desk so he could find the mouse. Vanessa was sprawled on the sofa with her legs sticking out over the side, her Psion organiser balanced on her knee and a glass dangling from her badly manicured fingertips.

'So what's wrong with the PC?'

'Somebody's been mail-bombing you.'

Vanessa glanced around the flat. It looked as if it had been gone over by the Scotland Yard computer fraud squad, with floppy disks littering the room and piles of print-outs of Usenet discussions.

'No, the place always looks like this.'

Norbert sighed, extracted his floppy disk from a puddle of Liebfraumilch and informed her that she'd been electronically mail-bombed. She wasn't getting any e-mail because her software was still busy trying to download several huge files.

'But I must get my e-mail. Men might be trying to contact me.'

Vanessa told Norbert that she'd spent the previous day posting a full-colour picture of herself (only slightly doctored with Adobe Photoshop to give a more faithful reflection of her true, inner self) to various different newsgroups: soc.personals, uk.singles, rec.dating and, on a whim, alt.fan.michelle-pfeiffer. 'I mean, I don't know why anyone should complain for chrissake... it's not as though I was spamming or anything.'

Norbert could think of several reasons why Usenet subscribers might object to photos of Vanessa being posted on the Net, but he kept most of them to himself.

'How big was the photo file?'

'Ooooooooh... say 80k? It would have been bigger but I cropped it just below my cleavage.'

'Yeah, but the only problem is that to save money some people download all the messages in the newsgroup at the same time,' said Norbert, 'even if they don't want to look at your picture. So they'll waste several minutes of phone time. Time is money. Especially if you've only got a slow connection. That's going to make them hate you.'

Vanessa was shocked. Why the hell would anyone not want to look at her picture?

'Suppose 50,000 Net-heads downloaded that file. That's a total of 150,000 minutes of download time – the equivalent of ten days hanging around in front of a screen. That's why there are special newsgroups for big postings like .GIFs and .ZIP files. High-bandwidth groups. They're the ones with 'binaries' in the title – like alt.pictures.binaries.dogs. Not that you'd want to post your photograph to that one', he added hurriedly.

Norbert explained that the huge backlog of files stopping Vanessa getting her e-mail was probably due to irritated Net-heads sending her multiple copies of her own file.

'To teach you a lesson. That's what passes for justice in the Net community. You'll be lucky if hundreds of geeks haven't forwarded the photo to your postmaster as well. That's the person in charge of your Internet services – he's got a lot of influence and you definitely don't want to annoy him.'

Vanessa raised a peroxide-coloured eyebrow and swung her legs off the sofa.

'Okay, shift. I need to use Eudora.'

She clicked the 'New Message' button and started typing.

```
To: postmaster@demon.co.uk
From: vanessa@blonde.demon.co.uk
Re: Binary File

Hi there.

I understand you may have received several
copies of the file 'VANESSA.GIF', a glamour
photo of me which I inadvertently posted to
certain Usenet groups.

I hope this has not caused too much trouble
- of course I shall do everything I can to
make amends.

So... how busy are you this Saturday night?

Mail me...

;-)

Vanessa
```

```
ps. I am attaching a copy of the file
VANESSA.GIF just in case you didn't get it.
```

Norbert was about to leave when Vanessa suddenly remembered why she had invited him over. She wanted to hire him to build her a Web site. As he packed away his floppy disks in their carry-case (£3.99 from PC World) she hastily poured him a drink and settled him down in front of the screen.

After a few minutes haggling he agreed to £375 plus his fares. This is good news for Vanessa because she is planning to bill the client for £3750. She knows that the client doesn't have a clue about what a Web site is, but the chairman's son somehow enthused his father, who instructed the marketing department to look into it. They would put up with any old rubbish – Vanessa was sure of that.

CHARLES AND VANESSA GET IT TOGETHER ON THE IRC

By 10.45pm Vanessa was feeling almost human again. She logged on to the IRC chat network. What if he didn't turn up? Being stood up in RL was bad enough, but being stood up on the Net? The way IRC (Internet Relay Chat) works anyone can join in, but the convenor of the channel can usually kick them off again. Vanessa went through the usual IRC setting-up procedure...

```
/nick vanessa).
/join #vanessa
/topic Waiting For Charles
```

...and waited. There were a few false alarms.

TexasTom Hi vanessa! whats charles got that I havent?
L-Vis hey babe are u lonesome tonite?

Then, at 11.15 – as she was about to fire off a pitiful e-mail

Charlie_S Vanessa! Help! How do I join a channel?
/msg Charlie_S Type /join #vanessa
Charlie_S has joined channel #vanessa
<vanessa> i was about to leave. i thought you'd stood me up
<Charlie_S> working late at the office. Never used this IRC before
<vanessa> youll get the hang of it. eventually.
TwelveInch has joined channel #vanessa
<TwelveInch> fancy a threesome?
<vanessa> piss off. its private
<TwelveInch> oooh I like forceful women
* TwelveInch bends over and asks vanessa to spank him
<Charlie_S> is Twelveinch your real name?
/kick TwelveInch
TwelveInch has left this channel
<vanessa> sorry about that there are some weirdos on here too
<Charlie_S> So tell me about yourself, Vanessa
<vanessa> well i'm blonde, 29, slim - what else do you want?

Bytes

>>> SUCK – FOR WEB SITES THAT.....

Suck is an invaluable hit list of Web sites you never want to visit — catalogues which pass themselves off as objective information and Netizens who bang on about their non-commericalism while adding their order form details to their signature file.

Aimed at 'those amusingly shady practices tying together journalism and sales'.

http://www.suck.com/

<Charlie_S> You sound like a harming woman
<vanessa> ?
<Charlie_S> oops I mean charming
<vanessa> hang on - just going to get a drink
<Charlie_S> What are you drinking?
<vanessa> white wine. just my small weekly glass.
Pete-L has joined channel #vanessa
<Pete-L> hey vanessa, long time no see
/msg Pete-L what are you doing here? go away
<Charlie_S> Is Pete a friend of yours?
<vanessa> no
/msg Pete-L i told you i wasnt interested
Pete-L Another guy eh?
<Pete-L> So, Charles, how long have you known young Vanessa? ;-)
<Charlie_S> She is going to India with me. I hope.
<vanessa> Have we met before, Pete?
* Pete-L laughs
<Pete-L> You wouldn't recall, considering the state you were in. BTW - I still have your tights in my airing cupboard.
/kick Pete-L
Pete-L has left this channel
<Charlie_S> What was all that about?
<vanessa> dunno. just some guy trying to wind me up. You get that on here if you

have a womans name. Tell me why you're single then Charles?
Goofy has joined channel #vanessa
<Goofy> Howdy
<Charlie_S> My wife died three months ago
<Goofy> Hallo from sunny California
<Charlie_S> in a freak yachting accident
<Goofy> What's goin' down in the UK then guyz?
<vanessa> Bugger off
<Charlie_S> Sorry?
<vanessa> Not you Charles
<Goofy> Only trying to be friendly
<Charlie_S> I was very distraught. Obviously. Its taken me a long time to get over her.
<Goofy> Anyone here like Benny Hill?
<vanessa> no
<Charlie_S> no
* vanessa shows Goofy the door
***Goofy's name is now BennyHill
* BennyHill walks into the door and slips on a banana skin
<Charlie_S> I have been a virtual recluse since I lost Linda. That's when I got into surfing the Internet.

<BennyHill> I have 2 other questions then. What is marmite and what is a wanker?
/kick BennyHill
BennyHill has left this channel
<vanessa> sorry charles you were saying? About Linda?
<Charlie_S> we were very close. 14 years of marriage. Her loss left this great gaping void in my life.
<vanessa> I know how you must feel. I split up with someone recently *and* he mistreated me. You still there?
<Charlie_S> Yes. I'm just getting a bit emotional here
<vanessa> dont worry I'm over him now
Pete-L has joined channel #vanessa
<vanessa> oh no not again
<Charlie_S> Have you ever done a CUSeeMe?
<vanessa> yes, I've got the I-connex eyeball camera. Shall we?

Vanessa switched on the camera connected to the computer and slid out of her shirt. Charles was going to like this!… Oh yes!

CHARLES' INTERNET SEX LIFE

For Charles, Vanessa had turned up at the right moment. After several days of scanning the Internet for sex and sex-related sites, Charles could honestly say that he was shagged out. He had learnt that a snake has two penises, that an average ejaculation of sperm contains a lot of protein but only 15 calories and that there is a World Masturbation Day. He also learnt that the Internet is a pervert's paradise.

Charles had started his sex tour of the net at 'The Complete Internet Sex Resources' site (http://sleepingbeauty.com/world/netsex.html). This has lists of sex links on the WWW, Usenets and gophers.

From here he clicked over to the World Wide Wank site ('the stuck together Web pages'), which can be found at (ftp://ftp.netcom.com/pub/ea/earl/WorldWideWank.html). Other categories include 'Things People Put Up Their Butts' (http://www.well.com/www/cynsa/newbutt.html).

Charles took the 'WWW Purity Test' (http://www.nmt.edu/~kscott/purity/purity.html), although anyone visiting this page was unlikely to be as pure as the driven snow.

He visited the 'Kama Sutra' (gopher://wiretap.spies.com/00/Library/Classic/kamasut.txt), which was rather drab as the publishers had made it a text-only site to conserve bandwidth.

'Girls on the Internet' (http://girls.com/home.html) was much more colourful. Donna first introduced herself and then invited Charles to meet all her friends. He skipped the introductions and went straight to Donna's Letters Page. He just had to see what the cyberpervs wrote in about…

```
'Dear Donna,
I find stockings and heels are a real turn-
on. Please tell me about yourself while you
are wearing them. I love your web page!
Malach

Dear Malach,
I tend to wear silky stockings with my short
tight mini dresses. But, I cover myself with
a coat when I go outside because last time
I went out in a mini with high heels and
stockings I caused a car crash!
Love and Kisses,
Donna'
```

'Oh Donna, you are style itself!' Charles said to himself. It was others who had sexual hangups, not Charles.

Next he went to the alt.tastelessness newsgroup, which styles itself as 'A newsgroup devoted to tasteless phenomena in all its forms. A place for people with a twisted and sick sense of humour. In alt.tasteless we like to get into the details … we want the feel of it, the smell of it, the stench of it, every little rotten and puss-oozing detail.'

Charles thought that was pretty gross. But it in no way prepared him for the huge variety of really sick sites that followed.

'Sexual Leftovers' (http://www.directnet.com/Crash/Purgatory/SexAndFood/Sex.html) caused him to make a sharp exit as his stomach just couldn't take the menu of weird sexual practices. He could handle the merely kinky (after all, he was pretty kinky himself), but not the insane. And autophagy – getting off on eating your own flesh – that was definitely not for the faint-hearted.

Charles considered going for some good, red-blooded, healthy sex at a virtual strip show (http://www.over21.com/ – you must be over 21 to become a member, and it costs), but he did not feel like paying. However, he was thrilled to find a solution to a little problem he was having with his current girlfriend, putting exactly what he wanted of her into words – and now here it was all neatly laid out for him at:

'Fellatio – Oral sex upon a penis' (http://www.halcyon.com/elf/altsex/asfaq_fella.html)

This answers all possible questions:
What is Fellatio?
What if it doesn't smell or taste good?
What is 'deep throating'?
Are there any special spots on the penis?
Should I use my hands?
What is '69'?
My boyfriend wants me to swallow. What do I do?
Can I make my seminal fluids taste better?
What are the contents of semen?

Feel like a sexpert now? Well, there's more: 'Helping Hand Guide To Sexual Techniques' (http://www4.ncsu.edu/eos/users/d/dczahn/www/totalsex.html). '…here's the good news: It's easy to learn how to be a terrific cock sucker. And I'm going to tell you exactly how.'

There were no diagrams or pictures, thankfully. But this know-it-all gave a blow by blow account of how to please your man.

'Sex Sex Sex Sex Classy Pictures Women Tits Pussy Fuck Phone Sex PROFESSIONALS' CHOICE. A Touch of Class Erotic conversation with sophisticated women. Imagine calling us… Then do it! (http://www.escape.com/ ~jaf/classy/classy.htm)'

Most sites charge a subscription fee for the really raunchy stuff. At Don's World (http://www.indirect.com/www/donald/adult.html) you can send off for the 'Wife Slut Course'. There are many requirements for those who want to partake (yes, we do live in a sad world, as if you needed any more proof):
'The candidate, after the proper indoctrination, must display an ability to be totally submissive to her husband sexually, and must furthermore display a hunger for that submissiveness. She must agree to be a 'slave' and for her husband to be her MASTER.'

dirty MACS

In Cyberspace everyone can be gay at least once. The opportunities for experimenting with sexual identity are too varied (and too safe) to be predicted. Taking on a new identity is as simple as changing your name in the communications software.

The Internet has until recently been a free zone for sexploitation. There was little or no censorship or regulation of any sort. Now the regulators are getting in on the act. Universities are altering their software to prevent students from concealing themselves behind false identitities. At Worcester College, Oxford, two male students had their Internet accounts withdrawn in 1995 after they e-mailed sexual messages to female students whose names they took from the college e-mail directory.

Even using a real name it is possible to conceal all sorts of characteristics from other Net-heads, like whether you are thin or good-looking or rich.

Video is now a possibility via the Internet, and the equivalents of mucky phone lines are burgeoning for the Net Generation as shoddy entrepreneurs with a box-room and a second-hand Quickcam realise it is one of the few ways of actually making money out of the Internet. One Califonian Internet video-sex company took $750,000 in its first four months. Punters dial in and give instructions to the girls in real time via their keyboards. The girls are paid $12 an hour.

'At 3 frames per minute over a slow dial-up connection and monochrome video she could look like Cindy Crawford's more attractive sister' thought Charles. In reality she looks like somebody's mother and is only working there because she needs the money. Which is not very much, but slightly more than one is paid just for chatting up sad, middle-aged men over the phone. The woman wears too much make-up despite the fact that the camera resolution is so low that it wouldn't look much different if she was wearing a gorilla mask.

She prefers this job to the ordinary phone chatlines because the clientele are less interested in asking her to perform bizarre acts with bits of fruit and more interested in drooling over how sexy the hardware is that enables them to see flickery video footage in real time. They frequently forget that they're supposed to be asking her to act out their sexual fantasies – until they get the bill for the four quid a minute usage charge.

GEEK AND NETROPOLITAN CULTURE CLASH

Howard was white-lipped with anger as he listened unbelievingly to the proposal that was being put to him. Yet again his puritanical morality was being insulted by a

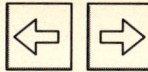

suggestion from a Newbie, albeit a rather sophisticated one.

Charles Netropolitan was visiting him in his capacity of MD of Four-poster Lingerie (motto: 'It's more fun in a four-poster'). The newbie MD wanted a legally acceptable Web catalogue for a range of clothing and marital aids goods – with thumbnail images that would lead to larger images if the browser wanted – featuring the top 50 of their 9000 lines.

Every attempt by Howard to explain that he just would not do that sort of thing was met with a refusal to comprehend on Charles' part. When he told Howard that he would not under any circumstances be involved in the advertising or sale of these things, the only reply was that the design of the Web site should be directed specifically towards achieving a high level of direct mail leads and requests for catalogues.

Charles wanted an adults-only registration form/acceptance statement that would lead on to various specialist rubber and bondage pictures for download, which he planned to sell for £2.50 a time.

What bugged Howard was that £1000 a day was awfully tempting.

VANESSA'S FAVOURITE SEX PAGES

Vanessa spent an hour looking before she found any Web sex for straight women – hardly surprising as there isn't much. But finally she found 'Jennifer's Naked Men Page!' (http://www.rpi.edu/~cearlj/naked.html), which had pictures of male hunks. Her favourite was Big Meat (http://www.rpi.edu/~cearlj/bigmeat.jpg). She nearly choked just looking at the picture!

Another good links page is 'Men on the Net' (http://www.contrib.andrew.cmu.edu/~nifty/men.html). This has links to about 10 sites ('Ten! Is that all?' Vanessa sighed). The world of the Internet is the same as the real world – women are not catered for when it comes to sexual material.

An e-mail answer to a question she put in a Usenet group was accompanied by a picture of four guys with erections. The most perverted thing she stumbled across was 'Mule Girl', a story that combined bestiality and paedophilia. It was a strange tale of a young girl – half human, half mule – who uses her appendage to whip her classmates into an erotic frenzy.

All sites warn on their home page if you are about to see material that may offend and inform you that if you are not 18 (or, sometimes, 21) you cannot enter – yeah, right?

Here's an example from Cadillac Richard's Adult Page (http://www.wolfenet.com/~cadillac/access.htm):
'This is a privacy wall designed to limit public view of "adult" material. You must be 21 or older to follow the link below. If you are under 21 years of age or do NOT wish to view adult material, GO NO FURTHER.'

This is just the kind of thing that would entice a young viewer to enter. The forbidden is always the most tempting.

For the really raunchy stuff you have to pay, and thus prove you are of legal age. But basic Page Three-style stuff can be accessed easily.

Something's got to give. Net-censorship will never work because the medium is international and countries will not agree on standards. The losers will be the big international providers who find themselves having to enforce the laws of the strictest company. Few of them are likely to set up in Saudi Arabia. Meanwhile we can surf the sex sites and amaze ourselves with how many freaks there are out there.

... I'M GLAD THAT YOU BEAR A STRIKING RESEMBLANCE TO PAMELA ANDERSON AS I BEAR AN UNCANNY RESEMBLANCE TO HUGH GRANT

Chapter 16

Tips for travelling with a computer

World telephone plug guide

Netropolitan travel sites

Surfing art on the WWW

Mobile Net

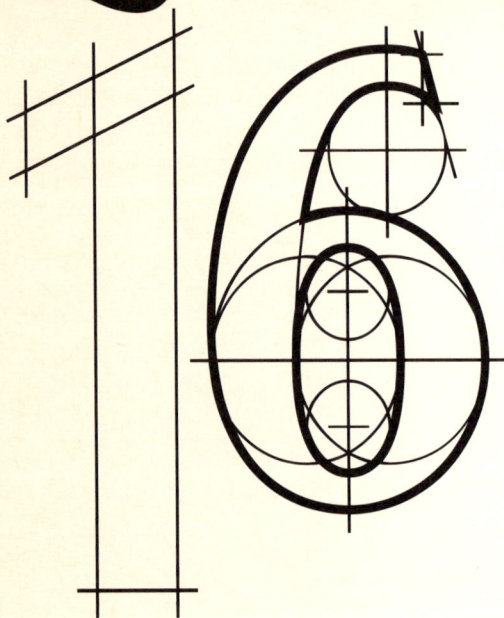

TRAVEL BY MODEM

TRAVELLING WIRED

Charles follows the advice he found in *Travels with a Laptop* by Michel Hewitt (International Thomson, 1995), which has tips and tricks for travelling with your computer.

The basic requirements for Charles' portable office are simple: a usable keyboard, a legible screen, a means of storing data securely over long periods and, of course, staying power; in other words, the batteries should last at least as long as a (subsonic) flight across the Atlantic.

CHARLES' WORLD TELEPHONE PLUG GUIDE
(Source: CompuServe)

The following is a guide to the telephone plugs that are used throughout the world. All developed countries have their own specific types, which have been adopted by other countries. The American plug – the US RJ11 – is the nearest to a 'standard' that exists and has been adopted in about 40 other countries – notably (outside of the USA and Canada) Greece, Spain and Ireland. Those countries listed as using the US RJ11 system are known to have it at least in the major hotels, if not throughout the country. In Romania, for example, the Intercontinental Hotel in Bucharest uses the RJ11, but older phones are hardwired. Travellers are cautioned that the US RJ11 is also used by modem and telephone manufacturers as a convenient quick-disconnect at the telephone base/modem body. Although this is identical and physically compatible with the US RJ11 telephone plug, electrical mismatches may occur if the normal telephone cable is removed from the modem and a locally bought cable is used, resulting in 'NO DIALTONE' messages.

Plug Types by Country

COUNTRY	ADVISED
ABU DHABI	British and US RJ11
AFGHANISTAN	Russian?
ALBANIA	Greek/Russian?
ALGERIA	French
ARGENTINA	Argentinian (2 types)
AUSTRALIA	Australian
AUSTRIA	Austrian – TeleFilter
AZORES	Portuguese
BAHRAIN	British
BANGLADESH	British (old) and US RJ11
BELGIUM	Belgian – TeleFilter
BELIZE	British and US RJ11
BENIN	French and S. African?
BOTSWANA	British
BRAZIL	US, Brazilian and French
BULGARIA	Russian
BURUNDI	S. African?
CAMEROON	French/S. African
CENTRAL AFRICAN REP.	S. African
CHAD	French
C.I.S.	Russian
CONGO	French
COOK ISLANDS	Australian
CUBA	Russian?
CYPRUS	British and US RJ11
CZECH REPUBLIC	Czechoslovakian – TeleFilter
DENMARK	Danish
DJIBOUTI	French
EGYPT	Turkish, French and US RJ11
ETHIOPIA	Italian
FAEROE ISLANDS	Danish
FALKLAND ISLANDS	British
FIJI	Australian
FINLAND	Finnish/Norwegian (2 types)
FRANCE	French
FRENCH GUIANA	French
FRENCH POLYNESIA	French
GABON	French
GAMBIA	British (old/new)
GERMANY	German (2 types) – TeleFilter
GHANA	British (old/new)
GIBRALTAR	British
GREECE	US RJ11 and Greek
GREENLAND	Danish
GUADELOUPE	French
HONG KONG	US RJ11 and British
HUNGARY	Hungarian

INDIA	British (old)	SAMOA	Australian
INDONESIA	Australian	SAN MARINO	Italian
IRAN	US RJ11 and Turkish	SAUDI ARABIA	British and US RJ11
ISRAEL	Israeli (2 types)	SENEGAL	French/S. African
ITALY	Italian	SINGAPORE	US RJ11 and British
JAPAN	US RJ11 and Japanese	SOLOMON ISLANDS	Australian?
JORDAN	US RJ11 and British	SOUTH AFRICA	S. African
KENYA	British (old and new), US RJ11	ST. MARTIN	French
KOREA (SOUTH)	US RJ11 and US old 4-pin	ST. PIERRE/MIQUELON	French
KUWAIT	US RJ11 and British	SPAIN	US RJ11 – TeleFilter
LEEWARD ISLANDS	US RJ11 and French/Dutch	SURINAM	Dutch
LESOTHO	US RJ11, British and S. African	SWAZILAND	British
LIECHTENSTEIN	German and Swiss	SWEDEN	Swedish (2 types)
LUXEMBOURG	German (old)	SWITZERLAND	Swiss (2 types) – TeleFilter
MACAO	US RJ11 and Portuguese	SYRIA	US RJ11 and Turkish
MALAWI	Danish and British/US RJ11	TANZANIA	British
MALAYSIA	British and US RJ11	TOGO	French
MALI	French	TONGA	Australian?
MALTA	British	TUNISIA	French
MARTINIQUE	French	TURKEY	Turkish
MONACO	French	UNITED KINGDOM	British
MONGOLIA	Russian?	VENEZUELA	Venezuelan
MOROCCO	French	YUGOSLAVIA	Yugoslavian
MOZAMBIQUE	US RJ11 and Portuguese	ZAIRE	Belgian/S. African?
NAMIBIA	South African	ZAMBIA	British
NETHERLANDS	Dutch	ZIMBABWE	British/S. African
NEW CALEDONIA	Australian		
NEW ZEALAND	British		
NIGER	French		
NIGERIA	British (old) and German (old)		
NORFOLK ISLAND	Australian		
NORWAY	Finnish/Norwegian (2 types)		
OMAN	British and US RJ11		
PAKISTAN	US RJ11 and British (old)		
PALAU	Australian?		
PAPUA NEW GUINEA	Australian		
POLAND	Polish/Russian		
PORTUGAL	US RJ11 and Portuguese		
QATAR	US RJ11 and British		
REUNION	French/Australian?		
RUSSIA	Russian		
RWANDA	French		

Countries using US RJ11

Antigua and Barbuda Bahamas Bahrain Barbados Bermuda
Bolivia Borneo Burma Cambodia Canada Cayman Islands
Chile China Colombia Costa Rica Cuba Diego Garcia
Dominica Dominican Republic Dubai Ecuador El Salvador
Grenada Guam Guatemala Guinea Guinea-Bissau Guyana
Haiti Honduras Iceland Indonesia Ireland Jamaica Jordan
Laos Lebanon Liberia Libya Malaysia Maldives Mexico
Montserrat Nicaragua Oman Panama Paraguay Peru
Philippines Puerto Rico Romania Seychelles Singapore Spain
Sri Lanka St. Kitts and Nevis St. Lucia St. Vincent Taiwan
Thailand Trinidad and Tobago Turks and Caicos Islands UAE
Uruguay Vietnam Virgin Islands Yemen.

Source: TeleAdapt, Gordon Brown
(100111.2713@Compuserve.com)

NETROPOLITAN TRAVEL SITES

Everybody with some kind of income travels, and Charles is no exception (naturally, his laptop travels with him). When seeking travel information on the Net it's easy to get lost as there are so many different travel sites. Yahoo has a Travel section, which you can search in (http://www.yahoo.com/). From here, the Net's travel resources are at your fingertips.

Charles often visits the Travel Resource Center (http://travelresource.com/index.html). He can also brush up on his foreign languages at Foreign Languages for Travellers (http://www.travlang.com/languages/). Choose Romanian, for example, and learn the crucial phrases 'Do you accept credit cards?', 'I'll buy it' and 'Bring me the bill'. Download the sound file and hear the tutor repeat the phrases.

Charles will be attending the multimedia fair in Cannes and needs to book a hotel. The place to start is the Accommodation Search Engine (http://www.netxtra.co.uk/accom/). There follows a form asking which services one would like: Bar, Wheelchair Friendly and even a service called 'Women Aware'! Charles finds this feature useful for checking hotels that are more likely to contain a high proportion of single women.

He decided not too rough it. Charles likes his creature comforts, so Intertrek (http://www.valnet.com/intertrek.html) was not for him. He pulled up two comfortable-sounding hotels in Cannes.

How many francs would he get for his dollars? He checked the CNN Currency News Page (http://cnnfn.com/markets/currencies.html) daily.

From Cannes Charles was travelling to Antigua with Caribbean travel specialists Air Travel (http://airtravel.com/ for more information). He was given a photographic tour of the Sandals resort in Antigua.

On the Info Hub WWW Travel Guide (http://www.infohub.com/) Charles accessed the Antigua and Barbuda page, which offered a room at the St. James Club.

The Yahoo Hotel Guide (http://www.hotelguide.ch/.) had the most comprehensive list of options. The Blue Water Beach Hotel sounded – and looked – great.

Then there was TravNet!, the 'International Home of CYBER-TOURISM' (http://www.sky.net/~eric/comdinet.htm.). Their Caribbean index is at http://www.sky.net/~eric/t/tni0007.htm.

Although the Internet is American, Cuba does get a mention. Try the newsgroup soc.culture.cuba, which leads to lots of other information about the country.

City Net is a service that lists Web sites with free information on 251 countries/territories and 570 cities online, and is starting to fund its operations through sponsorship.

The Whole Internet Catalogue and the Global Network Navigator from O'Reilly Press (both are obtainable from http://www.gnn.com) are very comprehensive information resource centres that contain links to sites in categories such as destinations, restaurants and leisure, accommodation agencies, traveller's reports and tourist guides. The resource centres are useful for travellers who are preparing for trips or researching trips directly with the information providers at the intended destination and have a heavy bias towards tourist, factual and anecdotal information sites.

The Virtual Tourist is an Internet Directory to the entire world's sites, which allows Net-heads to access Web resources relating to any information, including travel, by interacting with an intelligent world map and progressing down to country and, often, city level.

US State Department advisories on travel to all countries are available and are listed at several travel resource centres.

ART ON THE WORLD WIDE WEB

Howard and Carol like to surf the art on the Internet together. Their dream is the electronic equivalent of the nineteenth-century Grand Tour. Instead of a cabin trunk and a steamer, they use a computer and modem to tour the accumulated culture of western civilisation, gaining enjoyment as well as enlightenment from the journey itself and from the diversions that are to be found along the way.

From the pottery of ancient Rome to computer-generated graphics, everything that falls under the gargantuan umbrella of 'art' is lurking somewhere on the WWW.

The first port of call would be the Internet Art Resources site (http://www.ftgi.com/), where all the relevant links have been categorised and listed for easy access.

The Fine Art Forum Directory of Art Related Web Resources (http://www.msstate.edu/Fineart_Online/art-resources/) is a jumping-off place for people interested in the relationship between art and technology. This indexes hundreds of art resources that can be accessed via the Internet. Web sites, gophers, ftp sites, mailing lists and other types of resource are included.

The OTIS project (http://sunsite.unc.edu/otis/gallery.html) is a collaborative artist's site with everything from quilt-making to body art.

The Vatican has its own Web site where you can access the Cistine Chapel on http://www.christusrex.org/www1/sistine/0-Tour.html.

Most popular are the contemporary art sites on the WWW, some of which are listed below.

Contemporary Art Sites

Web Museum Network
  http://www.oir.ucf.edu/wm/
Chrysler Museum
  http://www.whro.org/cl/cmhh/
Morikami Museum and Gardens
  http://www.icsi.com/ics/morikami/
Centre du Georges Pompidou
  http://www.xs4all.nl/~gaud/org.htm
National Museum of American Art
  http://www.nmaa.si.edu/

Cyber Art Gallery Eindhoven
  http://asterix.urc.tue.nl/~rcrolf/cage/cage.shtml
Montreal Museum of Fine Arts
  http://www.interax.net/center/tour/mba.html
Art Crimes: Writing on the Wall
  http://www.gatech.edu/desoto/graf/Index.Art_Crimes.html
Andy Warhol (unofficial)
  http://www.altx.com/interzones/meade/shot.html
Andy Warhol Museum
  http://www.warhol.org/warhol/
Surrealism Server
  http://pharmdec.wustl.edu/juju/surr/surrealism.html
The Surrealist Imagery Page
  http://pharmdec.wustl.edu/juju/surr/images/surr-imagery.html
Dada and Surrealism, an online reference
  http://www.mercon.com/mercon/pyramid/edjames/surrdada.html
The Dali Virtual Museum of Art
  http://www.nol.net/~nil/dali/gallery2.html
The Dali Web
  http://www.highwayone.com/dali/daliweb.html
The Dali Homepage
  http://www.mercon.com/mercon/carl/dalilink.html

Art Newsgroups

Rec.arts.fine – A general-purpose art discussion group
Alt.art.com – A general-purpose art discussion group, no longer affiliated with the artcom group
Rec.crafts.beads
Rec.crafts.jewelry
Rec.crafts.marketplace – For the buying and selling of craft-related items
Rec.crafts.polymer-clay
Rec.crafts.textiles.quilting
Rec.crafts.textiles.sewing
Rec.crafts.textiles.needlework
Rec.crafts.textiles.yarn
Rec.crafts.textiles.misc – For textile-related discussions not covered by other groups in the rec.crafts.textiles heirarchy
Rec.crafts.misc
alt.surrealism

MOBILE NET

Charles wants to be able to check on his office workers from a holiday home in Guam. Using a Micro-AC inverter with a hire car he discovered he can run his laptop and printer, fax/modem, CD-ROM and scanner simultaneously with the use of a four-way plug. IBM has tested the product – which operates off 12-volt and 24-volt batteries – to its satisfaction. It is one of those rare things – a British invention that has not yet been sold lock, stock and barrel to the Japanese.

The Micro-AC inverter is available from Power Sciences at £59 plus VAT (a four-way plug comes free). Power Sciences can be contacted on 0181 571 7040 (phone) or 0181 571 7050(fax).

Hettie's
STUDENT TRAVEL LINKS

Most travel sites are aimed at independent and business travellers. But there are also package tours and cheap fares.

The budget/student travel sites tend to contain information rather than advertising. Here's what Hettie found useful:

Campus Travel (http://www.campustravel.co.uk)
No Shitting in the Toilet (http://www.magna.com.au/~travdude/)
T@P Online (http://www.taponline.com/tap/submit.html)
Julie Jett (http://www.hotwired.com/juliejett/jettmail.cgi)
Student and Budget Travel Guide
(http://asa.ugl.lib.umich.edu/chdocs/travel/travel-guide.html)
The Cheap Travel Page
(http://www.prairienet.org/~dbrown/travel.html)

NETIQUETTE...
THINK OF THE NET-HEAD AT THE OTHER END WHEN DESIGNING WEB PAGES

'Welcome To The New Intermulticorpo Conglomerates Website!'

...read Norbert in purple-and-yellow, flashing, 50-point text that ran off the edge of his screen. At least he assumed that was what it said – it was difficult to tell against the tasteful bright orange 'fiery inferno' background.

Contacting host:
http://www.intermulticorpo.com
Host contacted
Loading image: 5% of 200K

He sat back and waited for the image to load. It was a large picture of the company chairman reclining on a beach in Bermuda. That was the only 'link' on the page, so he clicked on it. The following page read:

Error: Cannot access http://www.intermulticorpo.com/businessplan.htm
File Does Not Exist On This Server

At the bottom of the home page was a line offering the advice: 'If you have any comments about this home page, e-mail them to intermulticorpo@delphi.com'

Norbert composed a lengthy message pointing out all the flaws in the design – the fact that the graphics took far too long to load, the text was virtually unreadable, the background looked awful and the links

didn't work.

He refrained, however, from criticising the chairman's tan. In the interests of diplomacy, he added: 'Apart from that, I think your page is great.'

He clicked on the Send button, and the e-mail disappeared into the bowels of the Internet.

Five minutes later it came back with the message 'Address Not Valid.'

Chapter

17

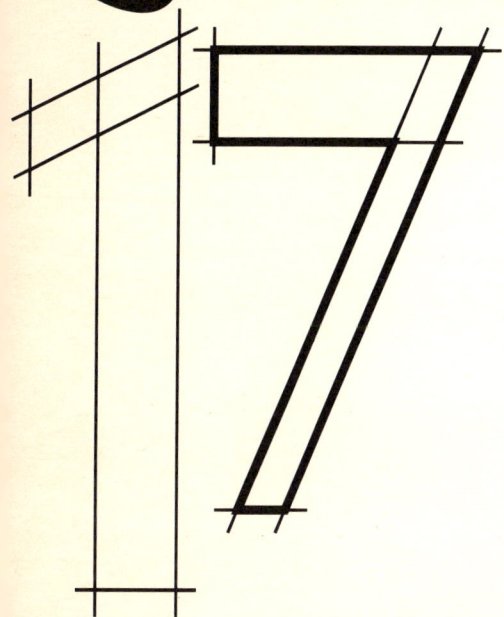

IS GOD A NET-HEAD?

God created the Universe and the Dataverse

Cardinal in Cyberspace

Malcolm searches the weird side of the Net

Have you ever been abducted?

World Wide Web of weed

Wackiest Web sites

Religious Web sites

Vatican online

God created the Universe and the Dataverse, and in many of the religious discussion groups He is seen as One of Us. The Net is infested with religious freaks, who post their bizarre philosophies to all@demon.co.uk, and the Scientologists, who recently paid £15,000 to have their Internet name registered in every country in the world.

If the Church only realised that the elderly are becoming Doom-heads because it beats watching Songs of Praise, they might put a vicar into Cyberspace.

MALCOLM THE CYBERPUNK GETS RELIGION

The Net attracts a higher than average proportion of crazies, Jesus freaks and other cultists. The combination of anonymity and a high concentration of lonely, inadequate people to prey on is the key factor. None of the really big TV preachers have gone online yet and there has been no e-mail sex scandal involving a member of the moral majority, but it can only be a matter of time.

In normal circumstances Malcolm treated them all with contempt, but he had not been feeling himself since swallowing a couple of unidentified pills at a party the previous weekend. He couldn't remember much about the evening, and since then he had been subject to occasional blinding flashes of multi-coloured light. He heard voices but assumed that they were coming from the computer speakers – which was strange because they had not worked since he had downloaded a 95-megabyte Heavy Metal file.

As a result, Malcolm's critical faculties were not fully operational when he came across the Alien Encounters page during one of his all-night surfing sessions.

'HAVE YOU EVER BEEN ABDUCTED ... had Alien Encounters? Are you an "abductee" or experiencer, without knowing it?'

'Millions of people, it seems, have had encounters with alien beings. Many of those do not realize that they are having these experiences because of suppressed memories.'

This seemed to fit his current symptoms with uncanny accuracy. Malcolm read the list of common indicators shared by most abductees:

'Ask yourself if you…
Have had missing or lost time of any length, especially one hour or more.
Have been paralyzed in bed with a being in your room.
Have seen balls of light or flashes of light in your home or other locations.
Have a memory of flying through the air which could not be a dream.
Have a "marker memory" that will not go away (i.e. alien face, examination, needle, table, strange baby, etc.)
Have seen beams of light outside your home, or come into your room through a window.
Have had dreams of UFOs, beams of light, or alien beings.
Have had a UFO sighting or sightings in your life.

Bytes
>>>SACKED FRENCH BISHOP GET'S DIOCESE– IN CYBERSPACE

French bishop Jacques Gaillot, who was sacked by the Vatican for his liberal views and given title to a Saharan diocese that no longer exists, has hit back by making himself the first bishop in Cyberspace.

Gaillot, a continuing thorn for Roman Catholic traditionalists, has begun preaching on the

Have a cosmic awareness, an interest in ecology, environment, vegetarianism, or are very socially conscious.

Have a strong sense of having a mission or important task to perform, without knowing where this compulsion came from.

Have had unexplainable events occur in your life, and felt strangely anxious afterwards.

Have awoken in the middle of the night startled.

Have awoken with marks, burns or bruises which appeared during the night with no explanation of how you could have possibly received them.

Have had, at any time, blood or an unusual stain on sheet or pillow, with no explanation of how it got there.

Have the feeling of being watched much of the time, especially at night.

Have seen a strange fog or haze that should not be there.

Have heard strange humming or pulsing sounds, and you could not identify the source.

Have awoken with soreness in your genitals which can not be explained.

Have had electronics around you go haywire or oddly malfunction with no explanation

Have insomnia or sleep disorders which are puzzling to you.'

It was eerie how accurately they had diagnosed him without even having met him, thought Malcolm. Maybe there was something to this UFO thing after all! Who knows, those in positions of authority usually had a few secrets up their sleeves.

WORLD WIDE WEB OF WEED

Occasionally Malcolm bumps into Hettie on his forays through the Internet's dark side. While he was checking out the legal situation as regards drugs in Holland, he came across her again, asking openly on one of the cannabis discussion groups about where she could score that night. That was a pretty stupid thing to do, and Malcolm's lip curled in disgust – this was no Cyberpunk!!

Hettie has been spurred on to risk her freedom by Natasha, who has also decided to skip the Jane Austen lecture in favour of cruising the Net. Sometimes Hettie wondered if her friends were more interested in the Net than in her.

Natasha had brought a little something to smoke. While she skinned up, Hettie tapped into the World Wide Web of Weed page (http://www.paranoia.com/maryjane/), where she discovered that White Widow Skunk had once again topped the cannabis charts.

The bush weed her friend was using was nowhere to be seen. Now puffing away, the two decided to access the Miramax cafe (http://www.dimensionfilms.com/cafe.html) and hang out there for a while. Then Natasha snatched the mouse and began to type in the URL for Antonio Banderas' site, http://www.sju.edu/~delvalle/antonio.html (which she had memorised), before they even got to the cafe. After swooning at Antonio, they decided to recruit him for their Legalise Hemp benefit gig at the college.

worldwide Internet computer network a year after Pope John Paul removed him as bishop of the Normandy town of Evreux.

The Pope ousted Gaillot, 60, for such acts as promoting the use of condoms to curb the spread of AIDS, allowing priests to marry and urging greater tolerance of homosexuality.

'Partenia', Gaillot's Internet Web page, which started up at the weekend, is named after the diocese the Pope gave him in southern Algeria as a punishment — an ancient, ruined city covered by the Sahara Desert since the Middle Ages.

He now has a potential congregation of tens of millions around the world.

http://www.partenia.fr

MARTIN'S WACKIEST WEB SITES

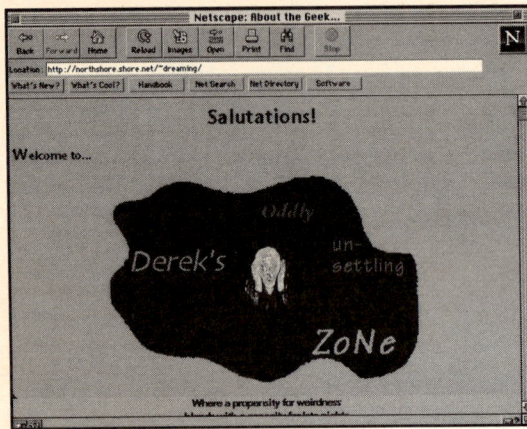

SEARCH FOR HITLER'S ANTARCTIC U.F.O. BASES
http://www.almanac.bc.ca/hweb/people/z/zundel-ernst/flying-saucers/expedition.html

BARRY'S TEMPLE OF GODZILLA
http://uptown.turnpike.net/~goldbergb/reviews.htm

MORMONISM
http://nowscape.com/mormons2.htm

PAN PACIFIC PAGAN ALLIANCE
http://sapphire.cog.org/other/pppa.htm

THE WORD OF LIFE SURFERS CLUB
http://www2.southwind.net/~wolreach/wolsurf.html
A group of people 'reaching out over the Internet with the good news of Jesus Christ'.

WELCOME TO FAITH CHAPEL OF THE INTERNET
http://webcom.com/faith/
The Church Without Walls…

HASTINGS UFO SOCIETY
http://hufos.sonic.net/hufos/intro.html
'Everyone here at the Society would like to welcome you to the 1st PSYCHIC CB RADIO STATION IN CYBERSPACE,

and I would just like to say thank you for taking interest in this IMPORTANT SCIENTIFIC EXPERIMENT.

'The Hastings UFO Society is strongly involved with the Sciences of UFOlogy, Alienology, and the Paranormal Sciences, and our Inaugural Psicast imprinted itself on the Hard Drive here at sonic.net.'

FLYING SAUCERS: THE BIBLE CONNECTION
http://zeta.cs.adfa.oz.au/KeelyNet/UFO/bibleufo.asc.html

The Scriptures suggest that Jesus' resurrection occurred when he was beamed up from Earth by a flying saucer. The three wise men probably followed a UFO to Bethlehem since stars do not move or abruptly stop in the manner the Bible describes.

MALCOLM'S LIST OF RELIGIOUS WEB SITES

FUNDAMENTALS OF ISLAM
http://www.coe.uncc.edu/~mlhutche/docs/fundamentals.html

BUDDHIST
http://www.wsu.edu:8000/~mikeman/work-http/Bevin/page3.html

JUDAISM
http://www.ort.org/anjy/a-z/

HINDU
http://rbhatnagar.csm.uc.edu:8080/hindu_universe.html

JAIN
http://www.wavefront.com/~raphael/jain/jain.html

DRUID
http://www.io.com/~curucahm/MUGWORT/mugwort.html

UNIFICATION
http://www.cais.com/unification/

ZOROASTRIANISM
http://www.zip.com.au/~porushh/tenets33.html

SIKHISM
http://www.community.net/~khalsa/

RASTA
http://www.escape.com/~rastaman/Roots.html

The Church of Jesus Christ of Latter-day Saints has announced
an official Web site at http://www.lds.org/

MORMON NEWSGROUPS
alt.religion.mormon, utah.religion

PAGAN
http://sunacm.swan.ac.uk/~paganfed/

CHRISTIAN THOUGHT
http://cedar.evansville.edu/~rp7/rel130.html

SCIENTOLOGY
http://www.theta.com/goodman/ministry.htm

CYBERPUNK IRC SESSION

On the Internet, authoress J. C. Hertz likes to be known as
'Belikan'. The tall Texan, who wrote the book *Surfing on the
Internet*, knows Cyberspace like it was her own home town.
She makes appointments to meet people on the IRC (Internet
Relay Chat) sessions and swaps lame repartee with the likes of
Tom Servo and other insomniacs.

The following is a real taste of what happens in these late-night
chat sessions. 'Belikan pages' means Belikan is calling the
interviewer (the author) to get online. Net-heads teleport in and

Bytes
>>>VATICAN ON-LINE

The Vatican has gone online and the
information superhighway — serving up the
Gospel according to the Internet — now leads
to the frescoed halls of the Papal palace.

The site, which went online on Christmas
Day, is still in a fledgling state and
offers only limited services so far. But
millions of people have 'visited' it in
little more than a month and an e-mail box
received some 4,000 messages while it was
open on a temporary, experimental basis.
A lot of people asked for prayers from the
Pope because of personal situations - and he
answered some of them, said Vatican

spokesman Joaquin Navarro-Valls. Hit the
site now and you will see a picture of the
Pope and two options: 'Communications from
the Holy Father' and 'News from the Holy
See'. Eventually all important papal
pronouncements and Church documents - even
encyclicals from previous papacies - will be
there. Vatican officials hope it will be an
asset for scholars.

And no - just in case you were wondering,
as one e-mail correspondent was - you
definitely cannot go to confession on the
Internet. The information superhighway still
stops at the thick velvet curtain of the
confessional box.

You will soon be able to find all that and
more by accessing

http://www.vatican.va.

out, greet each other and move around in the virtual space.

Belikan pages:
'OK. We're both in the same place.'

'We just had trouble realizing that.'

Belikan says, 'This is kind of a crowded place for conversation. It's like "Martin could hardly hear her in the crowded hubbub of Bob's restaurant…"'

Spectre teleports in.

Destana sighs, 'Thank you anyway, Joz.'

Belikan says, 'Hee hee.'

Joz hugs Destana.

Destana hugs Joz.

Spectre goes north to E. Testarosa Avenue.

Belikan says, 'OK, this is the meeting place of last resort.'
Belikan says, 'When all else fails, meet in the back alley of some MUD.'

Martin says, 'It's kind of interesting, though, the potential for intrigue. Like meeting in a public park.'

Belikan says: 'Pseudonyms and all. Espionage. Can you imagine, sometime in the future, two people who are being followed, meeting in some virtual hotel room?'
Belikan says, 'ZenMOO is pretty cool, sarcastic little stunt that it is.'
Belikan says, 'It's this virtual Zen rest stop. If you talk too much, it kicks you out.'
Belikan says, '"cheshire.oxy.edu 7777"' mm that's a bit conceptual.'

Devo teleports out.

Belikan says, 'Ah, Devo goes home. Tom Servo has a Smith Corona. Hard to find cartridges for it nowadays. Tom Servo much prefers Microsoft Word.'

Devo goes home.

Akasha teleports out.

Shenaynay nods to Tom Servo – 'Good Call.'

Belikan says, 'Oh, my friend Dean has this country-death-metal band. He's nagging me to be in it. He says it'd be really v cool to a have a chick lead singer.'

Shenaynay says, 'Country/Death Metal?'
Shenaynay hrms. Shenaynay sings the song on the radio… 'Do You Mind If I Stroke You Up…'

Tom Servo corrects Shenaynay, 'No, country-death-metal.'

Neworder teleports in.

Belikan says, 'Metal. A genre whose time has come. Say so. Tom Servo's cool cos he…'

Praziquantel hugs Neworder.

'…doesn't have to say say to say something.'

Tom Servo thing you say, 'so Tom Servo's cool cos he doesn't have to say say to say something.'

Neworder squishes Praziquantel!

Quiz

QUIZ: WHAT KIND OF NET-HEAD ARE YOU? (v. 1.2 beta)

Tackle this simple test to find out if you are a raw Newbie, a Net-cadet, a Geek, a Net-veteran, a Cyberpunk, a Profiteer, a Net-activist or even a Netropolitan.

Unless otherwise stated choose just one answer to each question.

1. When you are net-surfing, do you wear:
a) 'Baywatch' sweat-shirt and beach sandals
b) T-shirt advertising a computer software game
c) A headscarf
d) Gold jewellery with your e-mail address embossed on it
e) Green wellingtons
f) Mirrorshades
g) The shirt and tie you got last Christmas
h) T-shirt with the PGP encryption algorithm written in assembly code

2. If your modem breaks down do you:
a) Throw it out of the window
b) Borrow a friend's
c) Buy a new one
d) Call support and threaten to sue the supplier
e) Go panhandling to pay for a new one
f) Order a new one by credit card (not necessarily your own)
g) Get a spare out of the cupboard full of older, slower, but still serviceable modems
h) Convert your fax machine into a modem with bent paper clips

3. If you call your Internet Service Provider's technical support line do you:
a) Get confused by the touch-tone support line options
b) Realise you've unplugged the modem in order to make the phone call
c) Have your membership number ready
d) Reverse the charges
e) Forget your membership number but get into a really interesting conversation about veganism
f) Have your phone rigged so you don't pay charges anyway
g) Give a clear description of the problem, then get asked to call the experts at Microsoft/Apple/IBM/BT
h) Give a highly technical description of three possible problems and then find that the number they give you to call is in fact your own voice mailbox

4. If your computer freezes do you:
a) Yell at it
b) Call IBM and tell them you've found a major flaw in their software
c) Try and memorise everything on the screen because you forgot to back it up
d) Call support and tell them to fix it now
e) Light a couple of joss sticks and offer it a bowl of rice
f) Decide that it would look better sprayed matte black
g) Re-boot, rebuild the desktop and pray
h) Threaten it with a logic probe and a soldering iron

5. Late at night do you:
a) Have a drink and flame someone
b) Try to chat up women on the IRC
c) Try to chat up men on the World Wide Wank page
d) Video-conference a deal in Asia
e) Garner support for your 'Save our BSE cows' petition from around the world
f) Hack into foreign military computer systems
g) Sleep soundly, happy that your computers are backed up, virus-free and secure
h) Test out your Image Intensifier Sniperscope

6. When someone asks you what the Internet is, do you:
a) Hurriedly change the subject
b) Launch into a half-hour monologue on the Information Superhighway
c) Offer to get a bottle of wine and show them how it works 'back at my place'
d) Explain about the advertising and trading potential and offer shares in your new Net-venture company
e) Happily show off the sights and sounds (but not the smells!) of the Glastonbury festival
f) Connect up to a grainy CU-SeeMe video conference at a San Francisco SoMa club – can those body piercings be real?
g) Berate all the media hype and show how useful the Net is for serious research

h) Explain how the widget in a can of John Smith's bitter works

7. Do you access the Internet via:
a) British Telecom
b) School
c) Cable-TV phone
d) Cellphone
e) Telepathy/Ouija board
f) Red/White/Blue box via a public payphone
g) ISDN
h) Inmarsat Satellite phone

8. Does your hard drive contain:
a) A mass of files on the desktop not organised into folders or directories
b) Pirated Warez games and undetected computer viruses
c) Loads of software you've downloaded from the Internet but haven't had time to open
d) Encrypted XXXX GIFs for sale
e) The names and phone numbers of 200 journalists
f) Computer-virus source code and hacker philes
g) Loads of downloaded software you've painstakingly tested and classified
h) Multiple boot partitions: Linux and Windows NT beta

9. Which of the following Usenet news groups are you most likely to subscribe to:
a) alt.sex
b) alt.binaries.pictures.supermodels
c) uk.media
d) alt.business.import-export
e) alt.activism
f) alt.ph.uk
g) uk.jobs.offered
h) comp.lang.java

10. If you met someone IRL (In Real Life) with whom you had had Net-sex, would you:
a) Run a mile
b) Have real sex with him or her (or them)
c) Tell your shrink immediately
d) Check out to see if they were as sad as you thought
e) Call the police
f) Arrange the next Net-sex session over the infra-red links between your personal digital assistants
g) Offer to marry them
h) Ask them how they feel about a threesome with a big VAX, a flying helmet and a stick of celery

11. If you had to name a pet or your firstborn child after a Net word, would you choose:
a) Starfleet
b) Anette Head
c) Flame
d) William Gates IV
e) Archie
f) k00l
g) Anon
h) 3l33t

12. Where do you connect to the Internet from?
a) A Cybercafe
b) Your bedroom
c) Your living room
d) Your dedicated teleworker office at home
e) Your office phone line after you have unplugged the fax and answering machine
f) Anywhere with a phone line out of public sight
g) Your open-plan office cubicle at work
h) From your bed (you sleep with your computer)

13. How do you relate to the phone system?
a) You wonder who Bob Hoskins is always talking to in the BT ads
b) You quickly realize that you dial your Internet Service Provider more often than any other number in your 'Friends and Family' telecoms discount scheme
c) Friends and family have to contact you through IRC or e-mail as your phone is always busy
d) You rely totally on your mobile phone but are frustrated by the short battery life
e) You have set your computer to speed-dial your important contacts
f) You are never without your lineman's handset and crocodile clips and dream of fibre-optic connection tools
g) You have phone lines from three different telecoms companies to ensure that your systems are not out of action for too long as a result of 'leaves on the line' or the 'wrong type of snow' type disasters
h) You can remember your IP address but not your home phone number

14. What kind of computer system do you use to connect to the Net?
a) CD Interactive TV-top box
b) PC 486 clone running Windows 3.x
c) Apple Macintosh
d) IBM Thinkpad with Butterfly keyboard running Windows 95
e) Secondhand Apple Notebook with solar-powered modem
f) Stripped-down wearable portable with head-up display
g) Noname Taiwanese PC clone running Linux and X-Windows
h) DEC Alpha cluster with OpenVMS and go-faster stripes

15. What do you drink while surfing the Net?
a) Milk
b) Orange Tango
c) Instant coffee from a machine
d) Freshly roasted Blue Mountain Arabica

cappuccino
e) Camomile tea infusion
f) Choline-enhanced smart drink
g) Imported Czech lager
h) Jolt Cola

Answers

Mostly (a) You seem to be an inexperienced Newbie. There is no shame in this – everyone has to start somewhere. You may have skills and experience in other areas that you can bring to the Net.

Mostly (b) You are no longer a beginner, but you still have a lot to learn as a Net-cadet. If you are over 15 you have a problem and should consult a shrink.

Mostly (c) Netropolitans see the Net as an inevitable part of their work and leisure life. You may feel the urge to wash and wax your computer on a Saturday morning. Go with it! You still have a lot to learn but can relax in the knowledge that you are leading edge.

Mostly (d) There is money to be made as a Net-profiteer – who knows, perhaps you are the next Bill Gates and on your way to a billion or two. Just try to avoid these three words: 'Make money fast'.

Mostly (e) As a Net-activist you are an e-mail and Usenet addict, ceaselessly stirring debate among the chattering classes. In politics, nobody can feel the weight of an e-mail petition, but it is the activities of yourself and your fellow activists that will one day bring the Internet to a standstill.

Mostly (f) The accomplished CyberPunk treads the line between freedom and oppression. He/she may be a bit of a hacker or phone phreak, but more importantly the CyberPunk roams the Net with style. Your key mantra: 'Information wants to be free'.

Mostly (g) As a Net-veteran you bear the mental scars caused by the frailty and incompatability of software and hardware. Your expertise is rivalled only by the Geek, but you do have other redeeming social skills.

Mostly (h) As a Geek, you may be the expert in some important or merely obscure areas of the Net, but perhaps you need to leave your screen and keyboard once in a while and Get A Life!

Net-Head Booklist

Geek books

EXPLORING THE INTERNET – A TECHNICAL TRAVELOGUE by Carl Malamud
PTRPH Prentice Hall

MH & XMH E-MAIL FOR USERS & PROGRAMMERS by Jerry Peek
O'Reilly & Associates, Inc.

TCP/IP NETWORK ADMINISTRATION by Craig Hunt
O'Reilly & Associates, Inc.

LEARNING THE BASH SHELL – UNI SHELL PROGRAMMING – A NUTSHELL HANDBOOK by Cameron Newham and Bill Rosenblatt
O'Reilly & Associates, Inc.

C++ THE CORE LANGUAGE – A FOUNDATION FOR C PROGRAMMERS – A NUTSHELL HANDBOOK by Gregory Satir and Doug Brown
O'Reilly & Associates, Inc.

Net-cadet books

I DIDN'T KNOW I COULD DO THAT ON COMPUSERVE!
H&R Book Company

UK SCHOOL INTERNET PRIMER by Nicholas Mailer and Bruce Dickson
Koeksuster Publications

DOOM GAME EDITOR [THE HOTTEST SET OF TOOLS FOR BUILDING DOOM LEVELS] by Joe Pantuso
Net-Evangelist Books

INTERNET: MAILING LISTS edited by Edward T.L. Hardie and Vivian Neou
Prentice Hall (Internet Information Series)

Net-vet books
THE WORLDWIDE WEB HANDBOOK by G. Flynn
International Thomson Computer Press

ABCD … SGML – A USER'S GUIDE TO STRUCTURED INFORMATION by Liora Alschuler
International Thomson Computer Press

HTML SOURCEBOOK by Ian S. Graham
John Wiley & Sons, Inc.
('A complete guide to HTML/Create custom queries with CGI/Link text, graphics, video, and sound/Design Web pages for all browsers')

FOUNDATIONS OF WORLD WIDE WEB PROGRAMMING WITH HTML & CGI by Ed Tittel, Mark Gaither, Sebastian Hassinger and Mike Erwin
Programmers Press.
('CD-ROM features valuable source code plus CGI programming tools & utilities for the working programmer. Get complete coverage of forms-handling CGI, learn how to write a database front end, Perl, Java, Python, C, and UNIX shells')

INTERNET FILE FORMATS – FOR PCs, MACINTOSH, AND UNIX by Tim Kientzle
Coriolis Group Books
('CD ROM included – Your complete guide to understanding and using Internet files, provides inside information on the major file formats, includes the best tools for working with the Internet files')

THE DEFINITIVE RESOURCE FOR VRML TECHNOLOGY, VML BROWSING & BUILDING CYBERSPACE by Mark Pesce, foreword by Tim Berners-Lee
New Riders Publishing

THE USENET HANDBOOK by Mark Harrison
O'Reilly & Associates, Inc.

!%@:: A DIRECTORY OF ELECTRONIC MAIL by Donnalyn Frey and Rick Adams
O'Reilly & Associates, Inc.

Netropolitan books
E-MAIL ADDRESSES OF THE RICH & FAMOUS by Seth Godwin
Addison Wesley Publishing Company

THE INTERNET COMPLETE REFERENCE by Harley Hahn and Rick Stout
Osborne

THE WORLD WIDE WEB UNLEASHED by John December and Neil Randall
sams.net Publishing

USING THE WORLD WIDE WEB by Jim Minitel, Cheryl Willoughby, Heather Kaufman, Kelli M. Brooks, Noelle Gasco, Theresa Matthias, Jeff Bankston and Paul McIntyre
Que Quick Reference Series

MONDO 2000 – A USER'S GUIDE TO THE NEW EDGE by Rudy Rucker, R.U. Sirius and Queen Mu
HarperPerennial A Division of HarperCollins Publishers

USING YOUR ORANGE
Hutchison telecom

Cyberpunk books
MASTERS OF DECEPTION by Michelle Slatalla and Joshua Quittner
Harper Collins

SURFING ON THE INTERNET by J.C. Hertz
Abacus

REAL TIME by John Brockburn and Ed Rosenfeld
Picador

2600 THE HACKER QUARTERLY (various dates)
John Wiley & Sons, Inc.

Net-profiteer books
BUILDING YOUR OWN WEBSITE by Susan B. Peck and Linda Mui
O'Reilly & Associates, Inc.

INTERNET UK by Ivan Pope
Prentice Hall

BANDITS ON THE INFORMATION SUPERHIGHWAY by Daniel J. Barrett
O'Reilly & Associates, Inc.

NET GAMES: WHAT'S PLAYING IN CYBERSPACE by Kelly Maloni, Derek Baker and Nathaniel Wice
Random House/Michael Wolff and Co.

NET MONEY by Kelly Maloni, Nathaniel Wice and Ben Greenman
Random House/Michael Wolff and Co.

NET CHAT. WHERE TO MEET PEOPLE IN CYBERSPACE by Kelly Maloni, Nathaniel Wice and Ben Greenman
Random House/Michael Wolff and Co.

HTML & CGI UNLEASHED – EVERYTHING YOU NEED TO MASTER WEB DEVELOPMENT! by John December and Mark Ginsburg
sams.net Publishing
('CD-ROM includes powerful Web development tools, source code, templates, and graphics')

Newbie books

10 MINUTE GUIDE TO THE INTERNET
Kent alpha books

THE INTERNET RESOURCE QUICK REFERENCE by William A. Tolhurst and Mary Ann Pike
Que Quick Reference Series

NEW RIDERS' OFFICIAL WORLD WIDE WEB YELLOW PAGES 1996 EDITION
New Riders Publshing, Indianapolis

THE WHOLE INTERNET FOR WINDOWS 95 – USER'S GUIDE & CATALOG – A NUTSHELL HANDBOOK by Ed Krol & Paula Fergusson
O'Reilly & Associates, Inc.

THE COMPUTER USER'S SURVIVAL GUIDE by Joan Stigliani
O'Reilly & Associates, Inc.

UNDERSTANDING COMPUTERS AND DATA PROCESSING: TODAY AND TOMORROW WITH BASIC by Charles S. Parker
C.B.S. College Publishing

THE INTERNET GUIDE FOR NEW USERS

Daniel P. Dern
McGraw-Hill

POCKET GUIDES TO THE INTERNET, VOLUME 2: TRANSFERRING FILES WITH FILE TRANSFER PROTOCOL (FTP) by Mark Veljkov and George Hartnell
Mecklermedia

Net-head books

THE WHOLE INTERNET USER'S GUIDE AND CATALOG by Ed Krol
O'Reilly & Associates Inc./International Thomson Publishing

OFFICIAL INTERNET YELLOW PAGES by Christine Maxwell and Czeslaw Jan Grycz
New Riders Publishing

THE INTERNET YELLOW PAGES by Harley Hahn and Rick Stout
Osborne McGraw-Hill

THE ESSENTIAL INTERNET INFORMATION GUIDE by Jason J. Manger
McGraw-Hill Book Company

SPINNING THE WEB: HOW TO PROVIDE INFORMATION ON THE INTERNET by Andrew Ford
International Thomson Computer Press

THE MACINTOSH WEB BROWSER KIT by Dan Meriwether
John Wiley & Sons Inc.

GRAPHIC WORKS 1.1 – CREATIVE TOOLS TO PAINT, WRITE, EDIT AND PRINT PROFESSIONAL DOCUMENTS developed by MacroMind Inc. and Mike Saenz
Mindscape

Internet magazines

INTERNET (from EMAP Business Comms) edited by Neil Ellul – also deputy editor of *Datacom* – is £2.95 monthly. Issues include long and short (100 words) case studies, buyer's guides, opinion articles, etc. Aimed at high-end Net-heads and businessmen. Editor's e-mail address is: neile@computing.emap.co.uk.

NET MAGAZINE, £3.00 monthly from Future Publishing, is edited by Richard Longhurst. 116 pages long and aimed at low-end Net-heads. Tel: 0225 442244

THE NET DIRECTORY – £4.99 (occasional)

GET ONLINE – £4.99 (four issues a year). Complete guide to Internet access

THE WEB – £2.95 monthly. Tel: 01625 878888

NET USER – £3.95 (four issues a year). Aimed at younger audience

INTERNET & COMMUNICATIONS WORLD – published by Paragon

WHAT NET MAGAZINE? – WV publishers. Tel: 0171 485 0011.

Not on the newsstands

MECKLERMEDIA'S INTERNET WORLD – US edition sold over here

3W – the original Internet 'zine, edited by Steve Bowbrick and Ivan Pope. Contact: http://www.aol.com

Glossary
OF TERMS

Access Provider (also known as an Internet Service Provider or ISP). These companies are distinguished by their failure to answer the phone when their customers need help. They sell Internet connections, including software and dial-up home access.

ARPANET The first Internet, created by the Advanced Research Projects Agency (part of the US DoD) as the world's first indestructible defence communications network. It was to become the world's first indestructible pornography network.

Archie A free search service used to locate files and software over the Internet on remote computers. Archie may be an acronym – possibly for Acronyms Really Can Help Income from EEC

Bandwidth The maximum amount of information that can be carried by a telecoms cable. A 64k line ought to be able to carry 64k of data per second. In fact it can only receive at 1k per second because the Internet sure can be slow sometimes.

Baud rate The speed of transmission between two modems expressed as bits per second (bps). Anything less than a 28,800 baud modem is considered obsolete.

BBS Bulletin Board System. Like a private Internet. The biggest BBS companies, such as CompuServe and America Online, tried to make themselves into independent little prison camps on the Internet. Subscribers pay up to five times the cost of a direct dial-up Internet connection. But the public can only be fooled for so long and most are moving towards becoming Internet providers.

Bit Computers use binary language – a state of on or off represented by a single binary digit (1 or 0), which is abbreviated to 'bit'. One of the earliest sections of the Internet was called Bit-net. The New York artists who founded it

named it as an acronym for 'Because Its There'.

Browser A program to display and navigate the World Wide Web. Netscape had a huge market lead at the beginning of 1996, with as many as 90% of Net-heads preferring Netscape.

Client A program that requests services from another computer, called the server.

Data diddling Altering valid data in an unauthorised way – one of the most popular computer crimes. Found in University grade records or input records on bank transactions.

Data leakage Confidential data that are removed undetected.

Dial-up To connect to another computer by calling it up over the telephone network. Mostly you get an engaged tone.

Domain name A multi-part name that identifies an Internet computer, such as intervid.co.uk, which identifies a UK company called Intervid, or Harvard.edu, which identifies a US educational establishment called Harvard.

E-mail Sending and receiving messages by electronic mail is the most widespread, and least glamorous, use of the Internet. It is fast – and could be cheap if the cost of local phone calls was not so high.

Ethernet Local network system capable of supporting data transfer at up to 10 Mbits per second. Often used in offices to carry e-mail. Sometimes if the sender pushes the wrong button an entire office can read a private e-mail.

FAQ A frequently asked question (pronounced 'fack'). There are dozens of FAQ document that cover the basic information from a particular Usenet newsgroup or mailing list.

File transfer protocol (FTP) When you download a file, you 'FTP it' from a remote computer to yours.

Flames are electronic hate mail, frequently consisting of personal attacks against violators of newsgroup netiquette. The more wimpish the author, the more aggressive his or her flames are likely to be.

Gateway A point of connection between two or more separate telecoms networks. Also the name of a very top-end computer that all Net-

Heads would die for.

Gopher A menu-based system of searching the network for files.

Home page The main opening page of a Web site or document.

Host A computer that makes data available to other computers on a network. (How come it's not called a hostess?)

HTML Hypertext Mark-up Language – the programming language that's used to create Web pages. So easy a child could learn it in 30 minutes, which is why it takes adults about a week. HTML allows the creation of links between pages that are activated by a mouse click on a highlighted word.

HTTP Hypertext Transfer Protocol – the programming protocol that acts as an electronic agreement between computers, allowing them to connect to each other to form the Web. Most Web addresses start http://www... It is not necessary to type in the 'http://' part – which can save a lot of time if you're typing in lots of them.

Hypermedia Enables the display of a range of different media, accessible through hyperlinks. A World Wide Web page, for example, may contain photographs or drawings, textual formatting and links to audio and video soures.

Hypertext Data with links between separate elements that allow users to move through infomation non-sequentially.

Internet A world-wide network of computer networks communicating through a common language. The hard-wiring of the planet. Pretty amazing.

Internet browser The most popular browsers feature a graphical interface and point-and-click technology. Two of these are Netscape Navigator and NCSA Mosaic.

Internet Society Promotes the growth of the Internet and works to assist those groups involved in its use and development.

Intervid UK's wickedest Internet consultancy.

IP address An internet address expressed in numbers.

IP Internet Protocol on which the Internet is

based.

ISDN An Integrated Services Digital Network, which allows the communication of digital information at high speed over telephone lines.

ISP Internet access Service Provider (see 'Access provider')

LAN Local Area Network, a data network that serves only a local area, as opposed to a Wide Area Network (WAN). Hence the Net-Head expression 'Lan, Wan, Thank you ma'am'.

Leased line A permanent, open phone connection between two points. Net-heads who surf more than nine hours a day and pay for their local calls by the minute may find it's worth switching to a leased line.

ListServ Software that manages mailing lists by responding automatically to e-mail requests and distributing any messages to the entire list.

Logic bombs Programmes buried deep inside software and designed to cause havoc if a given event takes place. In one case a programmer who was expecting to be fired put a logic bomb into his company's personnel file so that all names would be erased if his was removed (it worked).

Lynx A text-only Web browser. Some actually prefer to surf the Web with no graphics. Don't they realise that's the reason it's so successful?

Mailing list A group discussion carried on through electronic mail, to which only members of the list have access. Often used for illicit communications, but equally often used by boring lawyers and accountants.

Mb A Megabyte, or 1,048,576 bytes. So now you know.

Modem Short for Modulator–Demodulator. Translates digital information produced by a computer into analogue sounds which can be sent down telephone lines. The receiving modem converts it back to digital form. Soon to be replaced by the set-top box.

Nameserver One of many Internet computers that lists Internet names and numeric addresses.

Netiquette The etiquette of using the Net. If you don't obey it you will be flamed (q.v.). The worst offence is sending unsolicited e-mail

advertising.

Net surfing Browsing the Net with no particular aim in mind. Employers call it 'time-theft' when their employees do it at work.

Network A system of computers that connect together to share programs, data, printers, etc. The Internet is effectively a worldwide network of networks.

Newsgroup A usenet discussion group. About 14,000 newsgroups now exist, each devoted to a particular topic, most of them appealing to an audience of a few hundred. But the most popular attract up to a million people a month.

Packet The basic unit of Internet data. A message is assembled into packets, each marked with the destination address and a number. The computer at the other end can tell if a packet fails to get through. It then sends a message to the sending computer asking it to send just that packet again.

Packet switching The process of sending packets through the network, allowing for alternate routing if a particular network link fails.

POPs Points of Presence – a local call rate Internet access point set up by an access provider.

PPP and SLIP Point-to-Point Protocol and Serial Line Internet Protocol. Protocols that allow home computers to connect to the Internet.

Protocol A protocol defines how computers communicate. It is a deal between competing systems on how they will work together to improve the reliability and speed of data transfer.

Router A black box on the Internet that determines which path Internet traffic will take to reach its destination. Cisco, which makes the most routers, is America's fastest-growing company.

Salami slicing Doctoring computer software so that micro-amounts of money are redirected from each transaction. The slices are so small that the loss may go unnoticed for years.

Scavenging Searching through rubbish outside megacorporations for old files with computer passwords and other details.

Server An Internet computer that makes data available to other computers across the network.

Signature file A note, usually containing your name and address and a brief quotation, that appears at the end of mail or newsgroup messages you send. 'Sig' files are supposed to be kept short, but many cannot resist including a favourite scene from Shakespeare or an ASCII graphic of Blondie the Bombshell.

SMTP Simple Mail Transfer Protocol. Used to transfer e-mail between computers; part of the TCP/IP protocol family.

Superzapping Most computers have software to allow the systems operator to restart the machine even after a serious crash. By accessing this programme unauthorised modifications could be carried out.

T1 or T3 Levels of high-grade, high-capacity phone lines. Many companies have T1 lines. T3 lines are found at a few big corporations, government and military facilities and within a phone company's network.

TCP/IP The set of protocols that determine how data are transmitted on the Internet. Transmission Control Protocol controls the transport of data, ensuring that they are delivered. Internet Protocol determines the packet structure of data and the addressing used to deliver data to their destination.

TELNET Internet software which allows you to log on to a remote computer as if your computer was inside that computer.

Terminal emulation Communication with a remote computer whereby your PC acts as a terminal connected to it.

Trapdoors Because programmers need to move around easily within their software they build 'trapdoors', which they remove before the software goes on sale. Sometimes they forget and hackers find them and gain access to a computer or data.

Trojan horse Adding instructions to software so it will seem to run as usual but will also perform unauthorised tasks, like reporting back to the author the activities the program is used to perform.

Twisted pair Two copper wires twisted around one another to reduce data noise.

Uniform Resource Locator (URL) URLs are the addresses of pages on the World Wide Web. These tell your Web browser to use the hypertext transfer protocol (HTTP) to connect to the desired address. URLs are entered in this format: http://machine.site.net/directory/subdirectory/file name.html.

User Network (Usenet) This network, which is accessible via the Internet, is the home of several thousand newsgroups that carry on active discussions on virtually any subject you can think of and some you can't even imagine.

VPOP A Virtual Point of Presence is a local call rate Internet access point set up by an access provider together with a telecommunications company.

Virtual Reality Immersive CyberExperiences. The last big thing before the Internet became the next big thing.

WAN Wide Area Network – connects LANs using private, national and/or international telecommunications networks.

Wiretapping Some transmission technologies, like satellites or cell-phones or normal domestic phones, are highly susceptible to tapping. Others, like fibre-optic cable, are difficult to penetrate.

World Wide Web (WWW, or The Web) An information space on the Internet unified by a common addressing system and containing a mix of text, sound, graphics and animation files which can contain links between each other even if they are on different servers (q.v.).

HOW TO USE YOUR FREE COVER DISKS
(Attached to the inside back cover)

INSTALLING THE ACCESS KIT SOFTWARE

To connect to the Internet, use the diskettes supplied and follow these steps:
1. Power up your PC and start Windows
2. Insert the IBM Internet Connection Services diskette 1 into your disk drive
3. If you are using Windows 3.1 or later, select File from the Program Manager. If you are using Windows 95, click the Start button
4. Select Run, then type a:/setup and click OK
5. Follow the instructions that appear on your screen
6. After installation is complete, remove the diskette from the drive and restart your PC

NOTE: If your diskette drive is not A, substitute the correct drive letter.

You get 10 hours free usage with these diskettes before billing starts.

REGISTERING FOR AN IBM GLOBAL NETWORK INTERNET CONNECTION ID

This ID allows IBM to track and charge for your Internet usage. The ID is also used to handle your electronic mail and is protected by a password. Be cautious about giving your password to others since anyone who knows your Internet User ID and password will be able to access the Internet and you will be billed. To open an Internet account, follow these steps:

1. After the software has been successfully installed, reboot your computer
2. Make sure that your computer is connected to your phone line
3. Click on the IBM Internet Connection icon, then the Registration and Support icon
4. Click on Open a New account
5. Click on Open a Personal account
6. Please read the IBM Internet Connection Service terms and conditions
7. In the Account Owner window, type your name, address, phone number and credit card number. Click on Next to continue
8. Next window, select a modem, registration dial phone number, dial prefix, comm port, and dial mode. Click on Next to continue

9. Choose your user ID, which will become a part of your e-mail address. You are allowed to enter a first, second and third choice. The system will attempt to give you the ID that you prefer unless it is already taken. Click on Next to continue
10. Click on Send Registration to IBM, then follow the prompts. Your information is sent via modem and your account will be established. The registration process returns your user ID and password in a matter of minutes
11. Once your ID has been created, write down the ID and password and keep them in a safe place

NOTE: When you register, your credit card information is sent using a secure private network. This information is not transmitted over the Internet.

CONNECTING TO THE INTERNET

To connect to the Internet, follow these steps:
1. Power up your PC and start Windows
2. Double-click the IBM Internet group icon
3. Double-click the Internet dialer icon
4. Click the Dial button (the IBM Connection Login window displays)
5. Enter your account ID, user ID and password and click on OK

NOTE: The login window disappears when you are connected. If there is a problem, a message displays

UPDATING YOUR SOFTWARE

Since we strive to provide the best possible service for our customers, we constantly upgrade the software and make it available for our users to install. Once you are connected, you will be able to download the latest versions of our dialer, phone list, and modem list. Here's how:
1. Click on the Dialer icon
2. Click on the Services icon
3. The IBM Internet Customer Assistance window will be displayed. Click on Update Software
4. Click on Download Latest Software
5. Choose the software that you want to download from the network
6. Once the software has been downloaded, disconnect from the network and restart your computer to ensure that the system changes take effect

For the UK IBM help desk call free-phone 0800 973000

Austria	0660 5180	Italy	1678 74770
Belgium	0800 71000	Luxembuourg	0800 2990
Denmark	8001 7400	Netherlands	06 0225670
Finland	08001 18010	Norway	800 11680
France	05 916050	Portugal	05055 3010
Germany	0130 829440	Russia	940 2000
Greece	00800 11931	South Africa	0800 9943533
Hungary	00800 11931	Sweden	020 791260
Ireland	1800 688100	Switzerland	155 5720
Israel	177 3532010	Turkey	00800 35390011